KITCHEN CHEESEMAKING

KITCHEN CHEESEMAKING

by Lue Dean Flake, Jr.

Stackpole Books

KITCHEN CHEESEMAKING

Copyright © 1976 by
Lue Dean Flake

Published by
STACKPOLE BOOKS
Cameron and Kelker Streets
Harrisburg, Pa. 17105

Printed in the U.S.A.

Library of Congress Cataloging in Publication Data

Flake, Lue Dean, 1943-
    Kitchen cheesemaking.

    1. Cheese.   2. Cheese—Varieties.   I. Title.
SF271.F55   637'.3   75-42117
ISBN 0-8117-2108-6

Contents

Chapter 1

Beginnings

People have many questions about cheese—what different varieties taste like, how to store them, how they are used, etc., but the biggest question is probably whether or not they can really be made in the kitchen. This question won't really be answered to your satisfaction until you slice into the black rind and golden interior of a Coon cheese or sample some homemade Cheddar toasted on a piece of black bread. Please bear in mind that until recently cheeses were made on farms and modern cheese factories have spent hundreds of thousands of dollars on the most advanced scientific equipment so that they can faithfully copy the cheeses turned out in the comparatively primitive farm kitchens of yesteryear.

In fact, the legends of antiquity tell us that cheese was discovered by accident. The story is that a traveler put some milk into a leather bottle made from the stomach of a calf before leaving on a journey. Several things began to happen immediately. The milk was ripened slightly by the bacteria normally present in milk, and rennin, an enzyme found in the calf's stomach, caused the milk to curdle. When at last the traveler stopped for a meal, milk had made its leap into immortality; it had become cheese. In some places today cheesemaking hasn't developed far beyond this stage. In places in Latin America, for instance, cheese is regularly made in hollowed-out logs. Most cheeses require more precision than this, however, in order to achieve delicious nuances of flavor. Before considering those differences or even a brief history of how they came about, some-

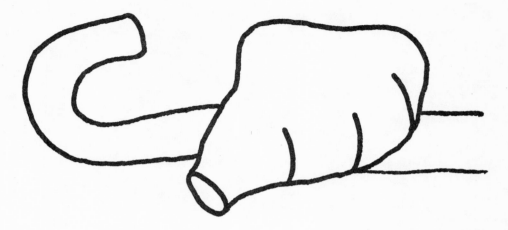

thing else—often ignored—should be mentioned: cheese's nutritional value.

Modern nutritionists have found that cheese is an excellent source of very high-quality protein. It contains the amino acids required for a proper diet and in almost the exact proportions needed. There is almost no waste; cheese is easily digested and is a good source of calcium and several vitamins. In addition, milk foods which have been acted upon by a starter are low in lactose. Those having lactose intolerance may eat these foods with relative immunity.

Scientists have been a little slow in their appraisal of cheese, perhaps because even a couple of thousand years ago the Greeks considered milk to be a perfect and superior food. That it indeed comes close was demonstrated with chilling clarity to the Western world by the Mongol hordes. Called among other things the "Divine Wrath," they were believed by many to be the embodiment of God's punishment. While Napoleon was defeated by supply lines stretched too far into Russia these nomads of the steppes would purposely ride north into the dark Russian winter, the land they called the "Land of Darkness," on raiding trips. For food on these ventures they carried a sort of dried cheese. About a half-pound of this was mixed with water every morning in a flask and the constant jarring of a day's ride would further mix up the contents, which they would eat in the evening.

The story of cheese runs like a thread throughout the records of mankind. From the fuzzy shadows of antiquity Homer speaks of it and it was ancient even then. David, historically recognized as king of Israel at the height of its power, was carrying cheeses among his possessions when he first heard of Goliath. Wealthy Romans enjoyed cheese along with other gastronomical delights such as hummingbird tongues. The monks of St. Gall entertained Charlemagne, the emperor of the Holy Roman Empire (which, incidentally, was not holy, Roman, nor an empire) with Roquefort. He was too polite to tell them the cheese had gone moldy so he picked out the blue veins until a monk told him he was missing the best part. From then on he ordered a number of the cheeses each year, stipulating that each cheese be cut in half, to be sure that the blue-green veins were there. Napoleon took time to name Camembert. One of the most famous cheeses was the Parmesan that Zoroaster, according to legend, lived on for years.

This volume concerns itself with the fermented milk products as well as cheeses. In many parts of the world the fermented milks replace cheese as a way of preserving milk and making a new and delicious product out of milk. Kefir has been little-known in the Western world due mainly to the fact that the Muhammadans kept knowledge of the sacred 'Grains of the prophet Muhammed' from the infidels.

The incredible thing about the cheeses and the fermented products is that while there are hundreds of different varieties, they all use the same basic ingredient. Some last only a few days while one Saanen, a cheese closely related to Swiss, was kept within a family for 200 years. One cheese was found in Siberia in 1948; it was 2,000 years old but still edible. Cottage cheese is soft, while it is rumored that an English train was once fitted with a set of Dorset Blue cheeses instead of wheels. Cheeses can be crumbly or have the resilience of rubber. The real difference between cheeses, though, is in how they taste.

Although the basic steps for making cheese will be discussed, this is just the beginning. The differences between the cheeses depend mainly on how and to what extent various cheesemaking steps are carried out. Depending on the kind of cheese desired, certain steps are sometimes omitted—in other cases new steps are added. As with a good many other things, the more often you make cheese the better they become. As the cheesemaker's competence grows, he will develop a feel for making cheeses exactly the way he wants them to be. Everyone develops their own style in going through the basic cheesemaking steps, and the milk used will be a little different from that used in other parts of the country, hence

the end product will probably taste slightly different. In fact, this is the way the great cheeses have come into existence. A good cheese is found and others try to copy it! Of course, there is always the chance that you could develop such a new cheese but, since the varieties are already of mind-boggling number, most home cheesemakers simply try to produce superior cheeses of already proven varieties.

Before making cheese, though, there are certain tools and utensils needed. There are also certain specific ways to carry out the basic cheesemaking steps—things you should know if you want to make really good cheese. The next chapter is concerned with these basics; by taking the time to become thoroughly familiar with them, there will be rewarding dividends in better cheeses.

Chapter 2

The Essentials of Cheesemaking

In spite of the bewildering variety of cheeses, their methods of manufacture are surprisingly similar. Before getting into the cheesemaking processes, however, some basic equipment will be necessary. As compared to the hundreds of thousands of dollars worth of equipment found in modern dairies, you will, I think, be pleasantly surprised, for you probably already have almost everything needed in your kitchen right now.

Thermometer: There are special dairy thermometers but a bulb type that registers from 50 degrees to 115 or 120 degrees (Fahrenheit) is fine. Remember that mercury is poisonous, so if you use a mercury thermometer don't break it!

Double Boiler: A double boiler that will hold at least several gallons is necessary. Any pan or container that will fit inside a larger one holding water will do.

Long-bladed Knife: The knife should be sharp and have a blade long enough to cut through the curd to the bottom.

Colander: You will need to strain the curds from the whey. A sieve is

Utensils and Equipment

DOUBLE BOILER

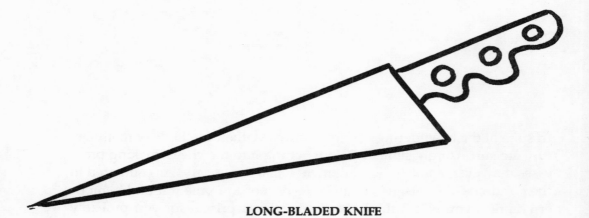

LONG-BLADED KNIFE

COLANDER

also popular. However, many home cheesemakers prefer the old-fashioned way and just stretch cheesecloth over the top of a pan and pour the curds and whey into it.

A Clean Hand(!): This is excellent for stirring the curd.

Cheese Mold: A cheese mold can be easily made from a clean tin can having smooth sides. The bottom and sides will have to be perforated with holes to allow the whey to drain from the curds. The holes must be punched from the inside or else the sharp, pointed metal edges of the

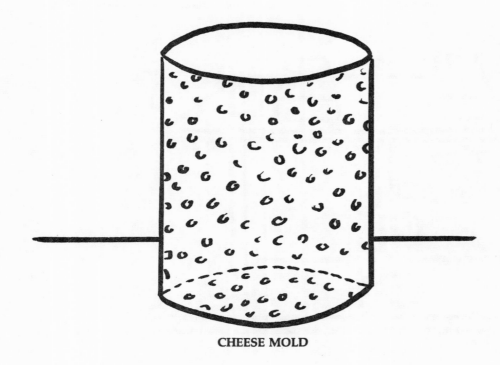

CHEESE MOLD

holes will catch on the cheese or cheesecloth, preventing its removal. To punch the holes from the inside is easier than it might first appear. Simply hold a short nail in the jaws of a pair of pliers, then tap on the pliers to perforate the holes. (The terms "cheese mold," "cheese form" and "cheese hoop" are used interchangeably in this volume.)

Follower: This is simply a disk cut out of hardwood or tough plastic. It must be slightly smaller in diameter than the cheese mold. When weight is applied to the follower, it presses moisture out of the cheese, compacting the curd.

Cheesecloth: Enough to line the mold and/or use from time to time as a sieve.

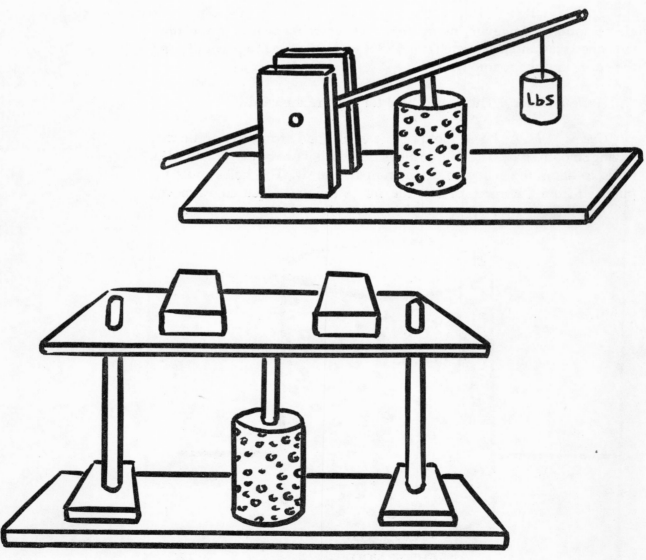

CHEESE PRESSES

Cheese Press: Several cheese presses can be homemade and even with today's inflated prices they should cost only a few dollars apiece for materials. The simplest way to press cheese curd is to put the curd in the cheese mold and add weight to the top of the follower. A small, perforated bread pan with a brick added for weight on top exemplifies this type.

The Basics of Cheesemaking

The cheesemaking process is not too complicated, as evidenced by the fact that cheese has often been produced by accident. After choosing the milk, a bacterial starter is added, and the milk allowed to sour or ripen. Then color is added, if wanted, and rennet to help it form a curd. The curd is cut in cubes, then cooked and drained. That done, the curd is salted, pressed in molds, covered with wax, then put aside to age and mature in a cool place. While this doesn't seem too difficult, things can go wrong. To help keep that from happening let's look at these steps one at a time.

Milk: Any type of milk can be used as long as it's of good quality; you just can't make good cheese from poor-quality milk! Choose milk free of disagreeable tastes and odors. Keep the milk and all utensils and containers as clean as possible. Do not use milk from animals that have been given antibiotics until several days after the medication has ceased. These antibiotics will show up in the milk and kill the starter, preventing the milk from ripening properly.

How much milk to use? There is really no set amount but the bigger the cheese, up to a point, the better the cheese, assuming all else is equal. The amount of cheese derived from a gallon of milk varies, but it is usually around a pound. A good general rule for the amount of milk to be used, taking into consideration the value of the cheesemaker's time as well as the quality of the cheese, would be perhaps two to four gallons for making some little-used or special-flavored cheese, and five to ten gallons for the basic, most-often-used type of cheese.

While any type of milk can be used, cow's milk is the overwhelming favorite for cheese. If you don't have your own dairy animals you can often get adequate supplies of milk from rural families or by advertising in a local farm paper.

Some cheeses call for pasteurized milk. There are two ways of pasteurizing. In the long-holding method, heat the milk to 143° F for a half-hour. In the short-hold method bring the milk to 162° F and hold that temperature for 20 seconds. With either method, heat the milk in a double boiler to avoid hot spots that might burn milk sugar and cause an off-flavor. After pasteurizing, be sure to keep the milk covered.

Ripening: This is the first actual step in the process of cheesemaking and it involves adding a starter to the milk to sour or ripen it. There are several reasons for this. One is to add an agreeable flavor to the finished product. Many microorganisms thrive in milk. To prevent undesirable forms of bacteria from developing, a known (friendly) bacteria is introduced which will produce good flavor and be safe to consume. As this bacteria proliferates, it develops acid which prevents other, possibly undesirable forms from growing. Its acid also helps form the curd and aids in the expulsion of whey. The recipes for the various cheeses in this book involve adding the starter and provide for a ripening period to follow. This will allow the milk to develop the proper amount of acidity for the particular cheese being made.

When the bacteriology of cheese is mentioned, some people have a tendency to get nervous. Just remember, though, that bacteria are merely plants not greatly unlike radishes or cabbages, but much smaller and more simple. When the starter is added, the cheesemaker is, in effect, planting seeds in milk which is already very fertile. After that all that is required is to keep the milk warm for the proper length of time and let the bacteria do the rest.

There are many varieties of bacteria that are suitable to grow in milk and which prove beneficial in cheese production. Some excellent cheeses have been made by simply allowing milk to ripen (sour) on its own volition. When undesirable bacteria forms are present, however, the cheese can be ruined, much as weeds can ruin a garden.

The problem of locating the proper types of starter culture for various cheeses is made unexpectedly easy by the fact that almost all the cheeses use the same basic starter, and to make it even easier, this is the same culture that is used in buttermilk. If you preferred, you could send off to one of the supply houses listed in the last chapter of the book and order a freeze-dried packet or vial of a culture, but why do that? Large commercial dairies do that periodically to assure a viable and active buttermilk culture. After all, they can't afford to take a chance with their quantities of milk. But just use a carton of their buttermilk to begin your starter. Be sure to rummage around in the back of the display case and get one from the very back. The fresher produce is put in the back and the older is pushed up front to assure a turnover of merchandise.

To make the starter you will need some milk to grow the starter in, and it must be free from bacterial contamination. Hence, for this "mother culture" it is best to use pasteurized milk. Since this starter will just be used for inoculating the milk, it isn't as important to avoid scorching the milk sugar as would be the case in pasteurizing the milk to be used for a cheese. Fill a pan with water and then put a couple of fruit jar lids on the bottom of the pan. Now fill several jars with milk. Skim milk is preferable and reconstituted dried milk works very well. Put the jars in the water on top of the lids to keep them from being in direct contact with the hot metal. Heat the water to just below boiling and leave the jars of milk loosely covered in the hot water for 20 minutes.

To grow the mother culture, cool the milk to 70° F and add a teaspoon of the buttermilk to a half pint of the sterilized milk. Cover with a lid that will not allow dust to enter and put it in a warm place overnight. The next day, when the milk starts to thicken, carefully taste it with a sterilized spoon. Care should be taken to assure that no microorganisms get into the container. The milk should taste a pleasant sour. Now add a teaspoon of the newly soured buttermilk culture to another half pint of the sterile milk. Allow it to set in a warm place until it also thickens and tastes distinctly acid. When this has happened take out three or four tablespoons of the buttermilk from the smaller jar and put in a quart jar of sterilized milk. Cover the jar and let it set in a warm place (around 70° F). After about 16 hours the milk in the bottle will have achieved enough acidity to form a curd (about 0.80%). Shake and stir to break up the soft curd.

At this point it will be at its most active stage and, if possible, should be used now. If this isn't possible, cool down the starter by putting the container in cold water and then refrigerate it until used. This mother culture will remain quite active for several days but will slowly lose potency. Long periods of refrigeration or allowing the starter to become too acidic is to be avoided. If any off flavors develop or the starter doesn't taste right at any of the above stages, it should be discarded and a new culture started, but this is not likely to prove necessary.

The starter can be used for some period of time. Just add some starter to some fresh milk the night before you are to make your cheese and then inoculate your cheese milk with it. Old starter can be used any way that buttermilk can be, so the riper the milk, up to a point, the drier the cheese. Then it goes mushy.

Coloring: Color has nothing to do with the quality of the cheese and its use is entirely optional. It is added for eye appeal only. If it is to be added to the cheese, it should be done before the rennet is added to the milk. Cheese coloring dye is extracted from the annatto tree and fixed in an alkaline base. If it is to be used for butter, it is fixed in cottonseed oil. Under certain circumstances small globules of fat escape coloring and so leave tiny white spots in the cheese. This seldom happens but if it does there is no cause for concern. Just make sure that the cream is thoroughly mixed into the milk in future batches.

Rennet: Rennet (available in liquid or tablet form) is added to the ripened milk, causing it to coagulate. How much rennet to use depends on how fast you want it to coagulate, and the size of the tablet itself. For instance, for two gallons of milk you would, under normal circumstances, use one-fourth of a 'Hansen's' cheese rennet tablet or three 'Junket' rennet tablets. The tablets should be crushed in a spoon, stirred into a glass of cool water and then added to the milk. Whether the liquid or tablet form of rennet is used, it is important that the rennet be mixed with at least 30 or 40 times its volume of cool water.

Add the rennet solution to the milk and mix it in well. Then let it sit in a place free from jarring or other disturbances until a curd of the desired firmness has formed. It is ready when you can pull the curd slightly away from the sides of the container. Another test is to push your finger into the curd, then lift up underneath it. If it breaks cleanly, it is ready. An average time would be from one-half to three-quarters of an hour. If the recipe calls for a short set, say 20 minutes, add extra rennet.

Of course the enzyme, rennin, isn't the only thing that can be used to cause milk to coagulate, but it's about the best and easiest. For information on alternate and vegetable rennets see final chapter.

Cutting the Curd: The curd will have to be cut into pieces so that the whey or moisture can be expelled more easily. Proceed as follows: Starting at one end of the container, cut the curd into parallel strips. Rotate the container 90 degrees and again cut the curd as before so that the surface is cut into squares. Now, starting one inch from the side, cut at a 45 degree angle under the curd. When doing this, follow the original cuts as closely as possible on the surface and repeat the process all the way across the top of the curd. When you reach the other side turn the knife at a 45 degree angle the opposite direction and again, following the original cuts, come back from the other direction. The curd should now be cut roughly into cubes. When doing this try to make the chunks of curd as nearly as possible the same size. The smaller the curd, generally, the drier and harder the cheese. The soft, moist cheeses are generally cut into larger cubes.

Stirring: Next, stir the curd for a few minutes. If you have missed a few pieces of curd on the angle cuts now is a good time to break them into smaller pieces so the whey will drain out of them properly. Many home cheesemakers prefer to stir with their hands because it gives best control.

Cooking: Slowly increase the temperature of the curds and whey in a double boiler. The rise in heat should be only about one degree every five minutes. Many find this the most difficult part of cheesemaking so here are some hints. Heat some water in a pan. Some of this water can be added to that in the double boiler to smooth out the temperature increases. This is especially useful on wood or electric stoves. Don't forget to use cold water to slow down the temperature changes if it is increasing too fast. If you prefer you can take some of the whey out of the pan, heat it and add to the curds and whey to regulate the temperature. By using this last procedure it is possible to slowly heat the curds and whey to the desired cooking temperature with no external heat source and no double boiler, if you so desire.

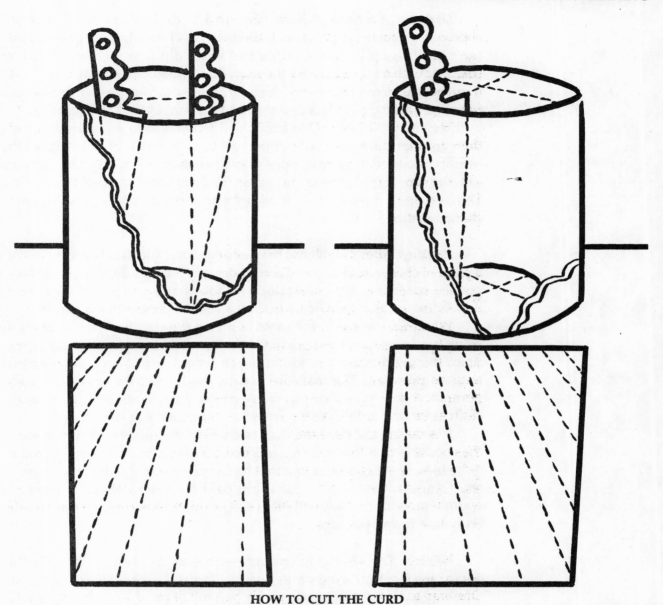

HOW TO CUT THE CURD

A. Starting at one end of the container, cut the curd into parallel strips. *B*. Rotate the container 90 degrees and cut the curd as before so that the surface is cut into squares. *C*. Starting one inch from the side, cut at a 45-degree angle under the curd, following the original cuts as closely as possible on the surface and repeating the process all the way across the top of the curd. *D*. When you reach the other side, turn the knife at a 45-degree angle in the opposite direction and again follow the original cuts.

The reason for the slow temperature increase is that if the curds are heated too rapidly a thin, tough film forms all the way around the individual curds. This film will prevent the moisture from being expelled. The result will be a watery, pasty curd that will become bitter and acrid. If you use a double boiler to heat the milk, keep the water level in the outer container as high or higher than the milk. Follow the directions in the cheese recipes as to temperature and how long the curd is cooked. It is very important to follow these directions carefully!

Draining and Salting: Next, the curd is drained by pouring into a cheesecloth, colander or sieve. If the batch of cheese is a big one and you can't lift it, simply dip the curds and whey out into the cheesecloth or colander with a sauce pan. By the way, don't waste the whey (liquid part); it can be used to make some of the whey cheeses. After the whey has been removed and the curd has drained, add the salt. Usually the salt is added in three equal portions. One third is added and then it is mixed in well, then another third, etc. Adjust the salt to taste but it ought to be in the neighborhood of three teaspoons of salt per gallon of milk used. The more salt, the slower the bacterial formation (and ripening) and mold formation. The real test, though, is if it is right to taste and has good ripening characteristics.

Pressing: After the salt has been added either line the cheese mold with a piece of cheesecloth or put the curd directly into the mold. You may also put the curds into the cheesecloth without putting them into the mold, depending on the specific instructions for the cheese being made.

When the cheese in the mold is put in the cheese press, start off by using light pressure, then gradually increase it to the desired level. Sometimes the instructions call for letting the cheese drain on a draining mat with no pressure. The mats are usually made of straw or reed, but any perforated flat surface can work. A cheesecloth, clean burlap or similar cloth stretched tightly over a frame or container works very well.

It is during the pressing that mechanical openings are often made. If the cheese is one that calls for mechanical openings, the curd should be quite firm. If the cheese is one that has a closed texture, the curd requires less firmness. One way to get a firm curd to close nicely is to press at a warm temperature. This will often soften the curd enough to form a solid body free from openings.

Waxing: The cheese is covered with wax to keep mold and other organisms from growing on its surface. It also keeps it from drying out. One way to wax a cheese is to melt a pan full of paraffin (wax) in a double boiler to almost the temperature of boiling water. Hold the top of the cheese and dip the lower half of it into the melted wax. Let it dry and cool for several minutes, then hold the waxed half and immerse the unwaxed half. Another method is to brush the melted wax all over the surface of the cheese. Always make sure that the whole cheese is covered.

Another alternative to waxing is oiling. The cheese is rubbed periodically with vegetable oil. Sometimes the cheese is periodically wiped with salt brine. Of course, not all cheeses are treated in these ways.

Ripening: Allowing the cheese to ripen depends on three factors; temperature, humidity and length of time the cheese is exposed to the other two factors. Probably the most important of these is the temperature.

CHEESE CHART

Milk Variety—								
quantity								
pasteurized?								
whole?								
Starter fresh?								
time added								
temp. when added								
Rennet how much								
time added								
Cutting when								
how big								
time start								
Cooking minutes per								
cooking temp.								
time stop								
Salt quantity								

Remarks:

Generally the temperature is held between 40° and 60° F. At temperatures lower than 40° F, ripening is inhibited and the cheese flavors often don't develop. At temperatures above this the ripening is very rapid and any bacterial defects are magnified, often resulting in acrid or off-flavored cheeses. Though there is a lot of fuss about maintaining proper temperatures, it isn't all that difficult. You can ripen the cheese in the refrigerator if the temperature isn't too low, a back bedroom or pantry, an outside building or root cellar. Take advantage of the weather to ripen certain cheeses as our ancestors did. If you would like, you can make a very well-insulated box to maintain proper temperatures, but an insulated ice box—the kind used to keep drinks, etc. cold on camping trips—works quite well too.

Humidity: Humidity is another factor that can be regulated to produce superior cheeses. Humidity, of course, doesn't greatly affect paraffinned cheeses one way or the other. But most cheeses require fairly high humidities to keep them from drying out; just put a pan of water in the ice box to provide that moisture. An alternative is to put the cheese on a small wire rack to keep it from touching anything, and put it all inside a plastic bag. Simply blow up the bag and then tie off the opening with a rubber band or piece of wire to keep it from deflating. For a high humidity, put a little water in the bag. This gives each cheese its own mini-environment. If you like you can put a hygrometer in the curing box. This will tell precisely how high the humidity is.

Now that we have discussed the basics you should be ready to move on to the actual cheesemaking. Follow the steps carefully and use the cheese chart to keep a record. It only takes a moment and will pay dividends. Don't be discouraged by a few setbacks, especially when trying a new cheese for the first time.

Chapter 3

Cheddar and Family

The flavors of cheese are widely varied and distinctive but when someone mentions cheese most people think of a fairly definite group. These cheeses are the subject of this chapter. They include two basic cheese types. Though they are related, they represent two of the ten basic categories of cheese as divided by the National Dairy Council. The cheeses in this chapter represent approximately two-thirds of all the cheese bought and used in the United States. In addition to the very familiar cheeses, this chapter includes some of the little-known or almost forgotten cheeses that belong to this same generic group. The result is a surprising range of flavors.

Stirred-Curd Cheese

Also called "Granular" cheese, this cheese is a very good one on which to practice the basic cheesemaking steps. It employs all the steps mentioned in the last chapter but has no added ones. The flavor is familiar and good. Perhaps this is one of the first examples of man's preoccupation with improving both the flavor and keeping qualities of cheese. You may be seeing more of this cheese in the future because experts feel it is one of the cheeses most adaptable to fully-automated plants.

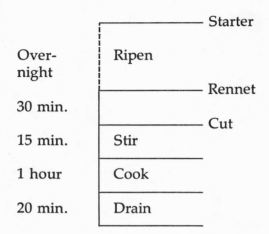

You will need:
    whole milk
    buttermilk starter (optional)
    cheese coloring (optional)
    rennet
    a cheese mold
    a cheese press

If you have access to fresh milk the traditional method is to let the evening milk ripen overnight at 40 to 45° F on its own and then add that to the morning milk. If you prefer, you can assure good bacterial activity by adding a teaspoon of buttermilk to the evening milk. Mix the morning and evening milk together. Slowly heat the milk and stabilize the temperature at 88° F. Crush the rennet and dissolve in 30 to 40 times its volume of lukewarm water. Mix the rennet solution thoroughly with the milk and—keeping the temperature at 88°—let it set without jarring until a curd forms that is firm enough to break cleanly over a well-washed finger or you can pull it away from the sides of the container slightly and it will retain its shape. It should be rubbery and firm. This should take about one-half hour.

Now cut the curd into ⅜-inch squares as explained in chapter two. Try to keep the size as uniform as possible but don't fret over the inevitable imperfections of your cutting, especially if this is your first try. After cutting gently, stir with your hand for 10 to 15 minutes to allow curd to expel whey and separate more easily.

Slowly, slowly increase the temperature of the curds and whey to 100°. Be careful not to go over 102° F. It should take you about one-half hour to reach this temperature. At the end of the first 15 minutes you should have reached a temperature of about 94°, maybe slightly less, but not more. The curd should be gently agitated through this whole process to assure that it doesn't mat together. As the cooking progresses the curd will become increasingly firm and the intervals between stirring can decrease somewhat. In the next 15 minutes continue to increase the temperature until it reaches the cooking temperature of 102°. Be especially careful not to let it fall under 98° F.

It is ready when you can wad up a handful of curd and it will not stick together. That will be in approximately one hour.

Dump into a colander and allow the whey to drain. In about 20 minutes, when the whey has slowed down to an occasional drip, dump the curds into a bowl or onto a board. Measure out the salt (3 tsp. per gallon milk) and add ⅓ of the total amount to the cheese. Mix in thoroughly. After it has been absorbed add the next third and repeat the mixing. Now add the last third and repeat the process as before.

Line the cheese mold with cheesecloth and dump the curds in. Fold the sides of the cheesecloth over until the top is covered neatly. Place the cheese mold in the cheese press and add a couple of bricks as weights. After an hour increase the weight and press another one to two hours. Take out of the cheese mold and rub with salt to keep down surface growths or with oil to keep the rind from drying out. Store in a cool place (about 45° F) until ripe enough to suit your tastes.

You may test the ripeness by cutting out a small triangular plug. With your thumb, nick about an eighth of an inch off the inner surface and taste.

Colby

Colby is an interesting variation of Stirred-Curd cheese. It is a sharper cheese that doesn't keep as well but ripens faster because of the increased moisture content. For those who like a good sharp cheese but don't like to wait for it, this is a good choice. Because it does have extra moisture, however, there is an increased chance of spoilage, though if you use a good quality milk and good starter the danger is small.

		Starter
30 min.		
		Rennet
30 min.		
		Cut
1 hour	Cook	
		Add water (extra step here)*
20 min.	Drain	

*The distinguishing feature of its manufacture is an extra step. It consists of adding cool water to the curds and whey after cooking. The result is extra moisture in the curd.

Since this is a fast-ripening cheese, either use milk with a minimum number of microorganisms or milk that is pasteurized. Adjust the temperature to 88° F. Add ¼ cup of active starter per gallon of milk used. Add it to the milk and mix thoroughly. Now let it ripen for half an hour at a temperature of 88° F. Crush the rennet tablets and mix it with a volume of water 30 to 40 times greater. Pour in the rennet solution and mix it for two minutes or until you are sure it has been mixed in well. Now let the renneted milk set for one-half hour. At the end of that time the curd should be sufficiently hard to break cleanly over the finger when it is inserted under the curd at an angle and lifted up.

Now cut the curd. This cheese is slightly unusual for a high-moisture cheese in that the curd cuts are still made ⅜ of an inch square, just as in Stirred-Curd cheese. After the cheese has been cut into squares, make the diagonal cuts that will cut them into cubes, as explained in the second chapter. After cutting, stir the curds with your hand for 15 minutes. This will allow the curds to firm slightly and start to expel whey. Slowly now, begin to increase the heat, stirring occasionally to prevent the curd from matting together. Time it so that at the end of 15 minutes the temperature will have increased six degrees. Now continue to increase the temperature for another 15 minutes. At the end of that time the temperature should be about 98° F. Stabilize the temperature at that point. Continue to cook the curd for another half hour or 45 minutes at that temperature. Continue to stir occasionally.

Notice that up to this point the whole process is very similar to that for Stirred-Curd cheese. Now comes a different and important step. If your kettle is full or almost so, ladle out some of the whey so that there will be additional room and add cool water slowly to the curds and whey. Keep a very careful watch on your cheese thermometer. Stabilize the new temperature at about 80° F. When that temperature is stabilized, slowly agitate the curds for 15 or 20 minutes. After initial stabilization the temperature will increase just slightly because of the heat retained in the cheese curd. It might be necessary to add just a little more coolish water to readjust the temperature. This extra step will increase the moisture content of the curd.

Now dump the curds into either a colander or cheesecloth so that the whey can drain off. If the cheese is to be a big one, dip the curds and whey into the colander with a saucepan until the cooking kettle is light enough so that you can pour out the remainder by hand. When the whey has by and large stopped draining, add the salt. Add salt at the rate of three teaspoons per gallon of the milk initially used. Add the salt one-third at a time and mix in well. When the salt has been mixed in and absorbed move on to the next step.

Line the cheese mold with a double layer of cheesecloth, then put the cheese curds in the mold. Since this is such a high-moisture cheese you might like to let the curds set for a few moments to let any additional moisture escape. Give it a shake or two to help settle the curds and then cut out a round piece of cheesecloth slightly larger than the diameter of the cheese mold. Put it over the top of the curds and tuck it carefully under the cheesecloth lining the sides. Keep it as neat as possible. Put the cheese-filled mold in the cheese press and put the follower on top. Add a small amount of weight at first and then, after a half-hour, add additional weight. Let it set in the cheese mold an hour to an hour and a half; then take the cheese out of the mold.

After the cheese has been removed from the mold it can be ripened. Melt some sealing or similar wax in a double boiler and when the wax is near the temperature of the boiling water dip half the cheese in it. Allow the cheese to cool several minutes and then, holding the cooled waxed portion, dip the unwaxed half into the wax so that the whole cheese is completely covered. If you would prefer not to wax the cheese excellent results have been obtained by rubbing the surface with olive or similar oil to keep the surface from cracking, or by rubbing fine salt on the surface to keep down mold growth. Besides being more work, these last two methods have the disadvantage of having to store the cheese in a moist room to prevent too much drying out.

Since Colby ripens so rapidly, it should be ripened at a rather cool temperature, but still above 40° F so that it will develop a cheese flavor. It is usually ripe after two to three months.

Cheddar is the most popular American cheese. It might interest those who like trivia to know that the largest single cheese on record was a Cheddar. It tipped the scales at 34,591 pounds!

American Cheddar

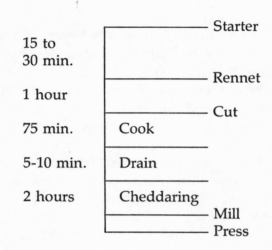

15 to 30 min.		Starter
1 hour		Rennet
		Cut
75 min.	Cook	
5-10 min.	Drain	
2 hours	Cheddaring	
		Mill
		Press

You will need:
  milk
  starter (buttermilk)
  rennet
  color (optional)

Cheddar is one of the more complicated cheeses but that doesn't mean that it is beyond the capabilities of the home cheesemaker. In fact, it was in the small dairies in the late 1500s that this revolutionary step was developed to counter unsanitary conditions and lack of adequate refrigeration. Because of these conditions milk often had high bacterial counts which sometimes produced off-flavored or fruity-tasting, gassy cheese.

In the cheddaring process the cheese is cut into strips which are piled and repiled on top of one another inside the cheese vat. The vat is kept warm so that bacteria from the starter can continue to develop at a high rate. When the cheddaring process is completed sufficient acid will have developed to kill the coliform bacteria that would cause it to spoil. During this process the elastic curd is also deformed, the small holes in the curd are pushed out and the characteristic Cheddar texture is attained. The moisture of the curd can be controlled at this point by how high the curd is piled, etc.

The milk can be whole or skimmed, but remember that most cheeses have less flavor when skimmed milk is used. In Cheddar's case the skimmed milk product loses the characteristic nutty flavor. If unsure of the cleanliness of the milk, you might also want to pasteurize it.

Warm the milk in the double boiler, stabilizing the temperature between 86° and 88° F. Add three tablespoons of starter per gallon of milk. Avoid high-acid starter or any other starter that might not be active. Use fresh starter that is known to be active and reliable.

If you are going to color the cheese add the color at this time. Mix well and let it ripen between 15 and 30 minutes. After mixing well, cover the kettle to keep it free from contaminating microorganisms.

Dissolve the rennet in 30 to 40 times its volume of clean, cool water. Add the rennet mixture to the milk and stir well for two to three minutes until it is evenly mixed. After the rennet has been thoroughly mixed into the milk, let it set for about an hour undisturbed.

After an hour the curd should have become sufficiently hard to break cleanly over a finger pushed at an angle under the curd and lifted up. It will also pull away from the sides of the container and retain its shape. It will have a certain elasticity, but will still break cleanly.

Cut the curd with a long-bladed knife into ⅜-inch cubes, as explained in the second chapter. If, after the first batch, you want to have a cheese with more moisture, cut the curd into slightly larger squares. By all means, though, try to keep the size as uniform as possible. Use a sharp knife to avoid breaking the curd. Using the knife, cut around the outside of the container to remove any curd that might have stuck. Be sure to scrape the bottom and sides so that no curds are left clinging to the metal of the pan.

To cook the curds, slowly increase the heat. Try to increase the temperature one degree every two and a half minutes. During this increase in temperature it is also important to keep agitating the mixture. Remember, too rapid an increase in temperature forms a film on the outside of the curd which will ruin the cheese.

After 30 to 35 minutes stabilize the temperature at between 98° and 100° F. Do not let the temperature go over 102°. Agitate from time to time during this holding period to keep the curd from matting together. The curds and whey should be kept at 98° to 100° F for about 45 minutes.

Drain the curd by pouring the curds and whey into a colander or through a cheesecloth stretched over the top of a container to catch the whey. By the way, you might want to save the whey for one of the whey cheeses described later on in this book. While the cheese is draining cover the curds with a damp, warm cloth or a piece of plastic to keep the curds from cooling off while draining.

After three to five minutes of draining, return the curds to the inner portion of the double boiler and put it back in the warm kettle of water (which should still be about 100° F). Spread the curds evenly on the bottom of the kettle and cover the container to keep it warm.

Now comes the process called cheddaring. After the curd has matted together sufficiently to be picked up, take the matted curd out and flip it over. The curd will also have exuded some whey and this should be either drained out or sponged up with a cloth. During the next two hours the curd should be turned over every 15 to 20 minutes and when there is an accumulation of whey, remove it. The temperature may be allowed to fall about ten degrees during this period. The main purpose of this extra step is to rapidly increase the acidity which will inhibit the growth of unwanted organisms. A side benefit is that the texture will also improve.

The next step is called milling. It consists of removing the curd from the container and cutting it into squares a half-inch or slightly more in diameter. Try to keep from breaking the curd into jagged, irregular pieces. Treat it as a ripe fruit; don't bruise it!

Next comes the salting, which is necessary to stop the rapid bacterial growth that has been occurring the last several hours. It will, to a certain extent, also dry the cheese out. Better results and a more thorough mixing of the salt and the curd occurs if the salt is added in three equal saltings. Add ⅓ of the salt which, in this case, is one teaspoon of salt per gallon of milk used. Then mix well, being careful not to bruise the curd unnecessarily. Repeat twice.

After the cheese is milled and salted it should be put in the cheese form and pressed. Line the cheese mold or form with cheesecloth and fill with cheese curds. Fold the top of the cheesecloth over the top of the cheese curds as neatly as possible. Put the cheese-filled form in the cheese press and slowly add weight. Only a little weight should be added at first to avoid bruising the cheese. Steadily increase the pressure and press the cheese at a high pressure for about 12 hours. After the initial pressing period, take the cheese out of the mold and let it dry four days. The cheese is paraffined by melting paraffin in a double boiler and then dipping one-half of the cheese in it. Let it dry for a few minutes and then dip the remaining half into the melted wax.

The cheese should be cured at about 45° F for three to six months. Depending on how sharp you like it and how much moisture is in the curd, which affects curing time, the time might be less or even as much as a year.

English-Type Cheddar

The English, or original Cheddar doesn't cut as well as the American type because of a more crumbly body. The flavor is sharper and slightly more salty. It can be prepared by following the directions for American Cheddar with a couple of exceptions.

During the cheddaring process allow it to cheddar in the warm pan for an extra hour. This allows the acidity to increase even more. This has an added advantage of cutting down the curing time for those who like a sharp cheese and gives some added protection against spoilage.

Coon

Coon is a very highly-flavored cheese liked by those with a taste for very sharp flavors. It is a Cheddar cheese that is cured in a special way. It is force-cured, so to avoid defects a good quality Cheddar is a must. Mold is allowed to grow on the outside of the cheese and then the cheese is plunged into hot wax which turns the surface black. Often extra cheese coloring is added to the cheese so that when it is finally cut open after curing, the black exterior is contrasted more sharply by the golden yellow or yellowish-orange interior.

The green (uncured) Cheddar should be bound tightly in the cheesecloth, but do not paraffin it. Put the cheese in a curing chamber at a temperature of between 60 and 65° F. The humidity should be very high to encourage mold growth, around 90 to 95 percent. Turn the cheese daily and wipe it with a cloth moistened in a mild brine. This daily wiping and the high humidity will keep the cheese from checking and splitting due to drying out.

The green mold that starts to develop should be allowed to grow. It is partially responsible for the unique flavor. When the mold has spread evenly and thoroughly over the surface of the cheese, it may be waxed. Heat the wax in a double boiler until the wax is the same temperature as that of the boiling water. Dip half the cheese in the hot, clear wax for three or four seconds and then take it out and let it cool for several minutes. Now repeat the procedure with the unwaxed half. The thick growth of mold will have turned a deep black.

Now the cheese can be set aside in the same warm 60 to 65° F curing room for the rest of the curing period. Continue to turn the cheese over every other day or so, so that it doesn't become deformed from being in one position too long. As soon as the cheese has been waxed the humidity ceases to be important so the cheese can be stored wherever that temperature can be maintained. Allow the cheese to ripen for around three months, depending on how sharp you want the final product to be. Because of the startling contrast between the rind and the interior, Coon is often served in thin slices on a cheese board.

Sage

It becomes increasingly difficult to obtain real sage cheese. Now it is common for the manufacturers to add sage extract for flavor. It still has the small green specks in it that look like chopped sage, but in reality it is often young, green corn, minced finely and mixed in the curd.

To make your own Sage cheese take two tablespoons of fresh, chopped sage and add it to one pound of cheese curd at the salting stage, just before it is hooped and pressed. The cheese may be Stirred-Curd or Cheddar. Mix in well and place in the cheese press and press it. Then proceed with the curing as you normally would.

Cheddar Club

Start with some Cheddar or Stirred-Curd cheese that is ripe and crumbly. Mash or grind the cheese up and then add some lactic acid (which can be purchased in health food stores). Taste the mixture as you add the acid until satisfied with the flavor.

Other sharp cheeses can be treated the same way. Pepper and other spices can be added according to taste. The taste soon deteriorates so use quickly.

Chapter 4

Soft Cheeses

There are many ways of classifying cheese. The cheeses in this chapter are the most popular of those with the outstanding characteristic of softness. There are two major differences in these. One is the texture; curd as opposed to a homogenous plastic mass. The other is the amount of butterfat in the cheese; ranging from skim milk to whole cream. There are other soft cheeses, of course, but Cottage Cheese (also called Pot Cheese, Dutch Cheese, or Schmierkase) is easy to make, good tasting, low in calories and high in nutrition. It sounds like a cheesemaker's delight, and it is. Besides that, it is an uncured cheese so it can be used immediately and all that is really required to make it is some milk. It comes in two forms: the large curd, low-acid form and the small curd, high-acid form.

Contrary to popular belief it is possible to use reconstituted skim milk with good results. It is imperative, however, that a starter be used when using dried milk. It is possible to use milk that has soured naturally until the necessary degree of acidity prevails but for better and more consistent results, use a starter. It is commonly lactic acid in the commercial creameries but, for the home manufacturer, yogurt or cultured buttermilk works just as well. A half cup of starter is added to one gallon of milk. This starter inhibits the growth of undesirable microorganisms and assures consistent, delicious results.

*Cottage Cheese
(Small Curd)*
(Farm or
Country Style)

Small-curd Cottage Cheese differs from the large curd in being a long-set cheese rather than a short one. This results in a smaller curd and a more acidic taste. In the commercially-manufactured, small-curd Cottage Cheese, a very small amount of rennet is added to speed up the coagulation of the curd. If home manufacturers follow this practice they must be very careful of the amount as too large an amount gives the curd a rubbery texture. If the 18 to 24 hours usually required seems a bit long and you want to make a medium-set Cottage Cheese, there is nothing to stop you from doing so. However, because the amount depends on so many factors it is impossible to give the exact amounts required. The thing to do is add a very small amount of rennet to the milk and starter mixture. Keep very careful records of time, heat, etc. You can then regulate it in the future until you find a length of time convenient to work with as well as a compromise in taste between mild and sweet, or sharp and acidy.

To make long-set, non-rennet Cottage Cheese you will need:
        skimmed milk
        buttermilk starter

Slowly warm the milk in the double boiler until it reaches a temperature of 72° F. Add ¼ cup buttermilk starter per gallon of milk and put the container in a warm place where it will remain at between 70° and 80° F. Cover the top of the container. (Clear plastic is nice so you can look at it periodically without disturbing it.) Let it set without disturbance until it has formed a smooth, rather firm curd. The curd should break cleanly over a finger inserted at an angle under the curd and then lifted up, but it shouldn't be brittle. The time, depending on conditions, is usually between 16 and 24 hours.

Using a long-bladed knife, cut the curd into ¼-inch squares, as described in the second chapter. Slowly heat the curds in the double boiler

and stir gently. Make sure that the water level in the double boiler is at least as high as the coagulated milk. Heat to a temperature of 110° F and hold there for 20 to 25 minutes, stirring every few minutes. If the curd still shows signs of frangibility, increase the temperature to 120° F but don't go beyond that. This should firm up the curds sufficiently. Drain in a colander or cheesecloth. When the curds have stopped dripping remove from the colander and add salt to taste and mix in well. Refrigerate until used.

Large-Curd Cottage Cheese

This renneted variety is also called "sweetcurd," "popcorn," and in some areas, even "flake." (The last name is discouraged by the author as it comes perilously close to using his name wantonly. The practice persists, however!) The curd is larger and sweeter and it takes less time to make.

You will need:
    skimmed milk
    buttermilk starter
    rennet solution

In the commercial preparation the milk is usually pasteurized and then cooled to the proper temperature. In the kitchen, especially when using pasteurized or reconstituted milk, the milk is heated carefully in a double boiler after the starter has been added. Slowly bring to a temperature of 90° F. Add one-fourth cup active buttermilk starter per gallon of milk. If the milk is heated too violently the starter will be killed.

Add about half the normal amount of rennet and stir well. It is important to mix the rennet with an adequate amount of cool water. The rennet's primary function is to set the curd at a higher pH, or—in other words—a sweeter and not so acidic state. It also gives the curd more cohesion and, later, when it is heated, aids in the expulsion of whey.

The temperature should be maintained at about 90° F for a period of about five hours. If you have trouble regulating the heat it is better to keep the temperature on the low side rather than the high side. A temperature lower than 90° F will merely increase the length of time before the curd sets and increase the acidity slightly. Too high a temperature will kill the starter or inhibit its growth.

When a smooth, firm curd forms across the top it is ready. Cut the curd into cubes about ½-inch in diameter as explained in the second chapter. Slowly increase the heat to cook the curds. To avoid a too rapid increase in their temperature it is often advisable to add a bit of extra water to the double boiler to help cushion the extra heat. Bring the temperature up to 110° to 115° F. Keep the curds and whey at this temperature, stirring every 4 or 5 minutes for 20 or 30 minutes or until satisfied with the firmness of the curd.

Pour into a cheesecloth-lined pot or colander and hang it and its contents up to drain by the four corners. Shift the curds when the whey slows to a slow drip by pulling harder on one corner and relaxing the opposite corner. When the dripping all but ceases put the contents, still in the cheesecloth, into a container of cold water. If it is over a sink, turn the cold-water faucet to a slow flow. With a spoon work the curd so that the water can freely enter in and around the curds, so that all excess whey will be rinsed away. Add salt, sea salt, pepper, etc., to taste and either use fresh or store in a cool place until used. Use as soon as possible.

Lactic acid is the precipitating agent of the more traditional small-curd Cottage Cheese described earlier but other acids can be used to clabber the curds as well. The juice from eight lemons (substitute limes, if you wish) added to a gallon of milk at about 72° F and kept at a warm temperature for from about 14 to 22 hours will give a new taste. Incubate, with as little disturbance as possible, until a smooth, clean-breaking but not brittle curd forms across the top. Cut into one-half-inch cubes and heat to between 110° and 120° F and let it sit for 15 to 20 minutes.

*Line a pot or colander with cheesecloth and pour the curds in. Hold by the four corners and hang over the sink or a container so that the whey can drain into it. It is desirable to change the position of the curd once or twice during the draining process to open any whey trapped in pockets of the curd. To do this, take down the cheesecloth containing the curds and pull one corner up two or three inches. This will roll the curds slightly in the cheesecloth, changing their position and opening the pockets of whey so that they can drain. Repeat with another corner toward the end of the draining process.

When the flow of the whey has ceased, immerse the cheesecloth and its contents in a clean container of cold water. Using a tablespoon, carefully work the curds so that the water can circulate freely among them and so that any excess acidic whey clinging to the surface of the curds is removed.

Season with salt, sea salt, pepper, or add a little cream, as your tastes dictate.

Lemon or Lime Cottage Cheese

Cottage Cheese, like the higher-calorie Cream Cheese, can be given a variety of tastes by adding condiments. Often the curd is a bit too dry for many tastes. In this case a small bit of cream is added to the finished curd and mixed in well. Cottage Cheese with 4 percent or more fat is called Creamed Cottage Cheese.

The flavor of Cottage Cheese lends itself to the addition of condiments

Variations

37

KITCHEN CHEESEMAKING

to enhance its flavor. Peppers, scallions, pimentos, olives and pineapple are favorites. Salt, sea salt, or pepper is commonly used.

The shelf life is about a week at 45° or 50° F but it can be frozen indefinitely at about 28° F.

Neufchatel

This cheese is very similar to Cream Cheese but has less fat content. As might be expected the flavor is not as pronounced as that of Cream Cheese. It is a soft cheese that should not be stored long as its keeping qualities are limited. Because of this the milk should be pasteurized to minimize the chance of spoilage. It is a whole milk cheese to which extra cream has been added.

Neufchatel is somewhere between Cottage and Cream Cheese in fat content. In the case of those having dairy animals, it can be made from whole milk to which the cream from the previous milking has been added. Over the years certain standards for percentage of fat, etc., have developed, but for all practical purposes this cheese can be made with whatever amount of butterfat you desire.

Use whole milk or whole milk to which the cream from the previous milking has been added. Mix the cream into the milk and add one-fourth cup of active buttermilk starter for every gallon of milk used. Mix the starter in well and then gradually bring the temperature to about 60° to 65° F. Add a small amount of rennet diluted with water and mix in well so that the milk will coagulate. After the rennet has been added set the milk aside overnight in a place where it will be about 60° F or maybe slightly higher. Make sure the container is covered so that no dust or contaminating organisms will get in.

Pour the solidified curd into a clean linen cloth and hang it up to drain. The edges of the cloth should be scraped down if any coagulum stops up the cloth and impedes draining. To speed things up you can use a large piece of cloth and tie the corners together so that it makes a big bag. You can then exert pressure on the bag to speed up the expulsion of whey. If the cloth plugs up, open the bag and scrape the thick plastic mass away from the sides of the bag with a butter knife or similar instrument. Turn this thick part back into the center of the bag so that the thinner portion can drain. When the whey has been expelled, the plastic curd can be taken out and salted. Like with Cream Cheese the salt should be added slowly and mixed in well. Add enough to focus the flavor and suit your taste.

Cream Cheese

Cream Cheese is a popular mild, rich, uncured cheese that is often used as a spread because of its soft texture. This cheese, like so many, can be made with or without rennet but it is best to use rennet. The cheese loses its

38

whey more readily, the flavor is often slightly better, and you will have a greater volume of the finished product.

You will need:
    cream
    rennet
    gallon container
    linen (fine weave or some similar cloth)
    buttermilk starter

Make sure that the cream is of good quality and has no odors or off-flavors. Stabilize the temperature of the cream at 60° to 65° F. Add two tablespoons standard starter for each quart of cream to be made into cheese. Make sure that the starter is mixed very well throughout the cream. Now mix up the rennet and add it to the cream. Make very sure that this is also mixed in very well. Now cover to keep out dust and foreign particles and set aside for 12 hours.

Just before proceeding to the next step, prepare the linen cloth. Make sure that it is absolutely clean. If it has been exposed to the air for only a few minutes it could have been exposed to contaminating organisms such as molds. One good way to sterilize it is to put the cloth in boiling water. If you add just a little bit of soda to the boiling water it will be sure to be sweet as well. Wring out the cloth and suspend it over a kettle or pan to catch anything that spills. Now pour the cream in. Grasp the four corners and it can then be held up like a bag. Tie the corners together so that the bag can be suspended over a pan or the sink. Every once in a while open the bag and, using something like a butter knife, scrape the inside of the cloth free of the solidified cream so that it will drain better. The plasticlike, solid portion should be turned into the middle so that the more liquid portions can drain. If you would like, you can trade off cloths. This will speed up the process. Just make sure to take the same precautions with the new cloth as taken with the old. Don't be discouraged if this takes longer than expected. Two days is about average. It can be speeded up, though, by scraping more often and changing cloths.

Something else that you can do if you're the impatient type is carefully tie the cloth into a complete bag so that no openings remain at all. Then you can put it on the drain board and put a weight on top. This will force the thinner whey out of the bag. The bag must be scraped often in this case, every time the whey stops flowing, but the process can be speeded up to a couple of hours.

When the bag stops exuding whey the cheese will be ready. By this time the cheese will be plastic, rather like modeling clay, but perhaps slightly thinner. Mix in well a small quantity of salt. Taste the Cream Cheese and add more salt until it suits your tastes. Make sure you add it slowly, though, so you won't get it too salty. The salt will make the cheese keep better besides adding flavor. Add enough to focus the flavor. Remember this is being made to suit your taste, no one else's.

When the salt is mixed in and dissolved in the body of the cheese, put it into molds. No weight is necessary, all that is necessary is to shape it. It is usually wrapped in four-ounce packages. Empty tuna fish cans make good molds. If it will be a week or two before you use it, you can retard mold growth by dipping the cheese in salt water before wrapping it.

Double Cream Cheese

Double Cream Cheese is a variation of regular Cream Cheese but a very thick cream is used. It can be renneted but, in this version, for contrast, we will use none. Cool the cream to 60° F. It may be desirable at this point to add just a little bit of salt to the cream to retard souring, especially in warm weather. Flake salt, if available, will dissolve more rapidly than conventional salt.

Pour the thick cream into a high thread-count linen or similar cloth suspended over a pan. Hold the ends together forming a bag. Either use a big enough cloth or a small enough amount of cream so that you can knot the ends of the cloth into a bag that will have no openings in it.

This cheese can be ready in as little as six hours. To speed this process squeeze the bag to increase the rate of expulsion of moisture and scrape down the sides of the bag regularly just as you did with Cream Cheese. When the cheese has obtained a plastic consistency, either mold it into the desired shape with your hands or press into a mold. Wrap in wax paper that has been wiped or dipped in heavily-salted water. This will retard the growth of molds that might want to grow. For a very interesting change in taste you can use Devonshire clotted cream in place of the heavy cream.

Chapter 5

Bacterial-Ripened Cheeses

This group of cheeses owes its flavor to amino nitrogen which is produced when the protein found in cheese breaks down. The bacteria responsible for this is *Brevibacterium linens*, the same organism that gives Limburger its flavor. Don't think, though, that all these cheeses are similar to Limburger, because they're not. The flavor intensity is determined by the amount of moisture in the curd, the surface area exposed to the *B. linens*, how much surface growth is allowed to grow, and the length of time and temperature at which the cheese is exposed to the ripening processes.

At the present time the bacterial surface-ripened cheeses do not enjoy a great degree of popularity in the United States although they are very well received in other parts of the world. Undoubtedly one reason for this is that the only *B. linens* cheese many Americans have been exposed to is Limburger, which is not only very strong but has often been allowed to over-ripen.

There are a couple of ways of introducing *B. linens* to the cheese. Perhaps the easiest way is to send off to one of the bacterial supply houses and buy the culture from them. The culture is added to a nutrient solution and then used to rub on the surface of the cheese. A faster way is to inoculate the cheese with one of the bacterial surface-ripened cheeses that can be bought in the grocery store.

Buy a small package of one of the easily procurable surface ripened cheeses such as Limburger or Brick. Then rub the surface of your recently-made cheese with the Limburger or Brick. When the bacteria has been introduced its growth and distribution is increased by what the people in the cheese industry call "smearing." All this consists of is moistening your hands with a little warm, salted water and then gently massaging or rubbing the cheese for 20 or 30 seconds. The bacteria already on the surface of the cheese will be spread about by this process. The object is to get an even growth of *B. linens* on the surface of the cheese. Even though the bacterial action occurs on the surface, through some process that we don't yet fully understand, the flavor spreads throughout the whole cheese.

An alternate method, and one used in the commercial dairies, is to rub the *B. linens* on the wooden shelves. This means that it is the shelves that carry the bacteria and when the cheese is put on them it becomes inoculated with the bacteria. The cheeses are then rotated every other day or so, so that a new surface is constantly exposed to the bacteria on the board. The cheese is still "smeared," though (as has been explained), to assure an even surface growth.

Bel Paese

This cheese is well adapted for making in the warm summer months. The lyrical name means "beautiful country" and while there are some attractive things about this cheese, it is best to get some experience with other cheeses first. In the high-moisture version this cheese ripens rapidly but keeps surprisingly well for a soft cheese. It can be made in a lower moisture version but the flavor isn't as good. However, since it does have better keeping characteristics the low-moisture version is the type you are most likely to be able to obtain commercially. In order to obtain good quality high-moisture Bel Paese you will probably have to make it yourself. Considerable latitude can be used in cooking this cheese and, since it is largely a matter of feel, this cheese is probably best made after a person has made other cheeses and developed a feel for the cheesemaking process.

Bel Paese is a trade name and not, as you might think, the name of a group of cheeses as is the case of, say, Parmesan. The cheese is certainly a youngster as far as cheeses go. It was evidently first made about 1890 and went big-time about thirty years later. Like most of the Italian cheeses it doesn't use the standard starter but, rather, a high-temperature starter made of the heat-loving organisms. It has one other peculiarity to consider before attempting to make it. This is the fact that it is surface ripened by *B. linens,* the same organism that gives the oomph to Limburger, though from a standpoint of odor—and for that matter, taste—it is a bit like comparing oranges and rhinoceroses.

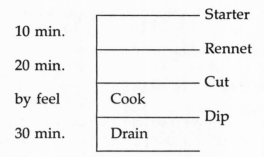

The cheese is very mild and, especially in the high-moisture version, good.

Besides *B. linens* you will need a different starter than that used for most of the cheeses in this book. In this case you can use yogurt. To help assure a good starter, make up a fresh batch the day before you plan to make this cheese. The starter should have a good flavor and reproduce rapidly. A fairly fresh start is recommended to assure that the *L. bulgaricus* and *S. thermophilus* are present in a 50:50 ratio. If the yogurt is old the ratio might be improper because one of the organisms has become predominant. Avoid old or very acidic starters!

The milk should be whole and if there is any doubt about the cleanliness of the milk it should be pasteurized. The milk for this cheese usually has right around 4 percent fat. The milk should be heated to about 107° F. When the temperature has been stabilized at that point or perhaps just a degree or two cooler, add the starter. You will need three tablespoons of yogurt starter for every gallon of milk used. Allow it to ripen at 107° F for 5 to 20 minutes. Then add enough rennet to the mixture to set the milk in about 20 minutes. Add perhaps just a little more than you normally would because the rennin enzyme starts to break down and lose effectiveness at these temperatures. When the curd has set sufficiently to break cleanly over a clean finger pushed under the curd at an angle and then lifted up, it is ready to cut.

Generally the curd is cut into squares ⅜-inch in diameter but they may be cut as small as ¼-inch for a dry cheese or as large as ½-inch for a particularly soft, moist, fast-ripening cheese. Be careful to make the cuts as uniform as possible. Particular care should be taken with the diagonal cuts to insure that there are no long strips left in the curds, but that they are all uniformly cubed. Cut the curd smoothly and rapidly.

Now comes the part that is so hard to put on graphs because so much depends on *feel*. On the other hand, one of the attractive things about this cheese is that you don't have to carefully increase the temperature to cook it. It is already at the cooking temperature. Maintain the temperature at about 107° F or slightly less and carefully stir the curd with your hand. It is very soft and easily damaged so just agitate it enough to keep the curd from sticking together. The length of time depends on several variables such as how large the curd was cut to begin with, the amount of acid developed in the whey and how dry or moist you want the finished product to be. The curd will gradually become more firm and little can be said about it except that when it becomes just slightly rounded and begins to firm up it is time to move on to the next step.

The curd is usually dipped into the cheese mold. In order to more easily facilitate this maneuver a colander or sieve is sunk into the curds and whey until it is about even with the surface. The whey will then flow into the colander and it can be dipped out without any danger of losing any of the curds. When the whey has been concentrated it is easier to dip out the remaining curds and whey into the shallow cheese molds located on top of a draining mat. The draining mat can be a traditional rush mat or one of perforated metal or plastic. The cheese-filled molds should be drained in a warm room at 75° to 80° F. Let the cheese drain for about a half-hour and then flip the mold over. In another half-hour again turn the mold over and then turn every hour for the next four or five hours. It is important that during this time the temperature is not allowed to fall too low. Try not to let it get below 75° F.

At the end of the draining period the cheese is salted by placing it in a brine solution. The brine needn't be a saturated solution but it should be almost that strong. As the salt dissolves more slowly in the water and it takes more and more agitation to dissolve it, you may stop adding salt. The brine is kept at a temperature of about 55° F. Put the cheese in the salt water and sprinkle salt on the top surface that isn't exposed to the brine. The cheese should be exposed to the salt water for about 15 or 16 hours depending on its size and the degree of saltiness preferred.

Up until now the flavor has been introduced by the starter added to the milk. In this cheese the lactic flavor is still there, but so is a subtle flavor of Bel Paese's own. First, it is necessary to move the cheese into a curing room having a temperature as close to 40° F as possible to maintain. The humidity should be fairly high also but it needn't be the oppressive damp needed by the mold-ripened cheeses. If you have some means of actually measuring the humidity, adjust it between 80 percent and 90 percent if possible. We still need it moist because this cheese requires quite a bit of care during this stage to prevent it from developing the stronger flavors of some other *B. linens* ripened bacteria. Another reason is that the cheese is unprotected by wax or oil, and without the protection of a high humidity it will dry out. When the cheese is introduced to the curing room there is no need to dry it off. Simply let it set in the curing chamber for a day or two and then introduce the *B. linens* to the cheese's surface.

The *B. linens* can be procured from a commercial source. If you prefer you can wash Brick, Limburger or some other cheese with a surface growth of this red bacteria in a very weak salt solution made from sterile water. Save this water to inoculate the Bel Paese cheese. A word of caution—the Bel Paese type of cheese has just a hint of flavor from this source and it is not unusual for other cheeses of this type to have, in addition to *B. linens*, certain yeasts. The purer the source, the less likely will be the chance of contamination causing off-flavors from these yeasts. The water containing the *B. linens* is rubbed on the surface of the cheese and allowed to grow, although during the rest of the curing period steps must be taken to keep the bacteria from becoming too prolific and causing too strong a flavor.

Unlike the other surface-ripened cheeses it is not advisable to ripen Bel Paese-type cheese on wooden shelves or boards that have been impregnated with *B. linens*. Instead, the shelves on which the cheese is ripened should be kept clean and the cheese should be washed and cleaned every other day. The bacteria will have a tendency to grow thickly on the surface. To avoid this and the pronounced flavor that comes with it, wash the cheese down with a mild, salty solution. If the surface growth is still pronounced, increase the salinity of the solution or else add a little vinegar to make the growing conditions more inhospitable. The slime that grows should also be partially removed during these washings.

The curing period, including the first several days before the *B. linens* are introduced, should last about three weeks. At the end of that period the cheese should have developed the mildly acid good flavor that distinguishes it from other cheeses. The red surface bacterial growth gives it a slightly different flavor that somehow penetrates all the way through the cheese. At the end of this period the cheese is ready to be paraffined. Melt enough wax to cover over half the cheese in a double boiler. Bring the water to a boil and dip half of the cheese in. Let it cool for several minutes and then dip the other half in. The cheese is ready to eat immediately. If it does come out with a bitter taste, it's probably because you tried to make the high-moisture cheese with too much moisture. It's best to start out with the low-moisture cheese, even though it doesn't taste quite as good, just to get the feel of it. When not eaten right away, the cheese is best stored in a cool place four or five degrees above freezing.

St. Paulin

In talking about St. Paulin, we are actually talking about a group of cheeses (St. Paulin, Le St. Paulin, Port Salut, Le Port du Salut), all practically the same, and made by the Trappist monks. Even though the distinctive flavor is caused by the same bacteria that gives Limburger its taste, there is a world of difference. First of all, many of the Limburgers bought in the grocery store have been allowed to ripen too much and are "wild," even for Limburgers! Second, the flavor is much milder, and that makes a world of difference. The flavor is mild enough so that it is palatable to almost anyone who dislikes strong flavors. It is mild enough so that it can be eaten in large quantities. But it still has enough flavor to give it a pleasing edge to

those who like to taste their food or who like to finish off a meal with a slice of cheese.

30 min.		— Rennet and starter
		— Cut
15 min.	Soak	
20 min.	Cook	
		— Drain
15 to 20 min.	Special Process	
		— Second Drain

46

You will need:
      rennet
      whole milk
      buttermilk starter
      open ended cheese molds
      1 to 2 gallons water (60° F) to which
         ½ cup salt per gallon has been
         added

Select a good-quality sweet milk with no off-flavors. If it is not pasteurized, do so yourself. Heat the milk in a double boiler until it reaches 165° F for a half a minute. Then cool the milk down to 90° F or, if the milk you are using is already pasteurized, heat it up to 90° F. Once the temperature is stabilized add the active buttermilk starter. Add two tablespoons of buttermilk starter per gallon of milk. Mix it into the milk well and at the same time add the annatto cheese coloring if desired. Immediately after this is done, add the rennet. There is no ripening period required for this cheese before the rennet is added. Add enough rennet so that the curd will set up and be sufficiently hard to cut in half an hour.

Carefully cut the curd into cubes ⅜-inch in diameter as explained in chapter two. After the curd has been cut, leave in the whey at 90° F for ten minutes. The curd will start to expel some of its whey during this time. Slowly increase the heat so that the curds and whey will gain about one degree every four minutes. At the end of fifteen minutes try to have increased the temperature to 94° F. Now stabilize the heat and allow the curds to remain in the whey for another five minutes. Before the end of the five-minute period allow the curd to settle to the bottom of the inner vat or pan. Agitate occasionally just enough to keep the curds from matting together.

Now quickly pour the curds and whey into a colander or sieve. Only allow it to remain in the colander for five or ten seconds or until the major portion of the whey has drained off. Don't make any attempt to drain off all the whey, just the bulk of it. Now dump it right back into the cooking container and immediately pour the salt solution that has been kept at 60° F. Now agitate in the salt solution for 15 to 20 minutes.

You may either dip the curd quickly into the open-ended cheese molds or pour it directly in. The cheese molds (or hoops, if you are using them) should be placed on a drain mat or on a tilted drain board. Let them set until about the same time the next day at room temperature, not in a hot room, just one that is cool and comfortable. Add no weights to the cheese. Just let it mat under its own weight. Now place the cheese in a brine solution and sprinkle salt on its upper surface. The next morning, or 12 hours later, turn the cheeses over and sprinkle salt on the top. During the salting in the brine the cheese should be kept at about 45° to 50° F.

The next day they will be ready for inoculation with *B. linens*.

Commercially, the cheese is often washed with salt water containing *B. linens* but you can use the smearing method if you prefer. Put in an area where it is very moist to cure. If you like, you can put the cheese in a large plastic bag with a little moisture in the bottom, blow up the bag and put the cheese on a clean board or rack which will keep it from actually coming in contact with the water itself. Keep the temperature around 60° F and turn the cheese daily. About every fourth day rub the cheese surface down with just enough moisture to moisten. On the 14th day of curing remove any surface growth that has accumulated by washing with a damp, coarse cloth like burlap. Leave in the curing room or box for two weeks.

Wipe all the moisture off and let it dry for five or six hours at room humidity. The more humid the room, the longer you will have to let it dry. Next, dip one-half of the cheese in hot paraffin for a few seconds. Take it out and let it harden. Then repeat with the other side. Traditionally, this wax is red. Now let it ripen for a couple of weeks in the refrigerator or at about 40° F. This cheese is not a particularly good keeper and it should be eaten within two or three months.

Muenster

This is one of the surface-ripened cheeses, like Limburger, but much milder. It is one of France's great cheeses, made first in or near the little town of Muenster, near western Germany. Now it is made through all of Alsace. Actually it is quite similar to Brick cheese, but it is softer and ripened to a lesser extent.

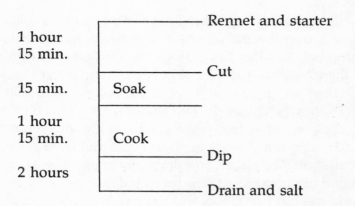

You will need:
  whole milk
  buttermilk
  color (optional)
  B. linens

Start only with good, sweet tasting milk of the best quality. Pasteurize it by heating to 165° for a half-minute and then cool to 90° F. When the temperature has been stabilized at 90° F you may then proceed. Add six tablespoons buttermilk starter per gallon of milk. Mix it in well and then add the annatto cheese color if you so desire. Add the rennet to a half glass of luke-warm water so as not to cool the milk down and add it to the milk. Stit it in very thoroughly. No ripening period is necessary before adding the rennet. Set aside in a warm place or leave on top of the stove. Be sure that it is disturbed as little as possible. In 20 or 25 minutes a curd should have formed. Let it continue to sit for one hour and 15 minutes after the rennet has been added.

With a long-bladed knife cut the jellylike curd into small cubes. They should be between ¼-inch and ⅜-inch in diameter. With the small size of the cuts it is easy to run over into the area you have already cut into strips. Avoid this, if possible, and make sure that no abnormally large pieces of curd remain. After the curd has been cut, allow it to settle in the whey for ten minutes. During this time agitate just enough to keep the curd from sticking together.

Though you will notice on the time chart at the beginning of this recipe that you cook for an hour and 15 minutes, the cooking is of a very gentle sort. Slowly increase the temperature. You will want to average just about one degree every four minutes. After 15 minutes check and see if you have reached 94° F. During the next 15 minutes continue to increase the temperature at the same slow rate until it reaches 98° F. During this time, agitate enough to keep the curds from sticking together. Notice that the curds will probably become just a little more buoyant and the more they are cooked the firmer they will become and the less tendency they will have to stick together.

During the last 15 minutes of cooking turn off the heat if you like and dip about two-thirds of the whey out of the inner pan, but leave enough to still cover the curds. An hour and 15 minutes after starting to cook the curds, ladle the curds out of the inner pan directly into open-ended molds or hoops. Have them on a tilted drain board or draining mat so that the whey will run off without collecting in puddles. Fill the hoops or molds completely. Do not add curd to them later as the curds compact. Let them drain undisturbed for half an hour and then flip them over so that the weight of the curd will push from the other end every 15 minutes for an hour and 15 minutes. Then let them set at room temperature for about four hours or slightly more if the room is cool.

Prepare a salt solution in some cool water. Take the cheese out of the molds or hoops. Sometimes the cheese sticks; if so, just run a knife blade around the edges to loosen it. Now put the cheese in the salt water. If it doesn't float, add some more salt until it barely does. Sprinkle some salt on the upper surface. Turn daily and repeat the salting for a couple of days. Don't let the room and the water get too warm! Keep the temperature at about 50° F.

Put the cheese on its side in a room about 60° F and as moist as you can get it. Smear the surface daily for four days with *B. linens*. You may do this by rubbing the cheese against another cheese, such as Brick, Limburger, etc. that has a surface growth of these bacteria, or you may rub it on a board that has been thoroughly smeared with this bacteria. With a little warm, slightly salty water, smear and work the bacteria all over the surface of the cheese. Use just enough moisture to dampen the surface as explained at the beginning of the chapter.

These cheeses traditionally have an orange rind. This is added by the cheese factories by drying the surface of the cheese off after the initial curing period, then mixing oil with annatto coloring and then rubbing it on the rind. Let the cheeses ripen for four weeks at 50° F for a mild flavor. For a stronger, more pronounced flavor, let them ripen accordingly longer.

Brick

Not only is the United States the world's largest producer of cheese but, despite its late start in becoming a country, it has still managed to develop a number of new cheeses. One of these is Brick cheese. This semi-strong-flavored cheese was developed in Wisconsin by John Jossi of Richwood. He developed it while he was operating a Limburger factory. The cheese was made about the size and shape of a brick but the name probably comes from using a brick as a weight to press the cheese. The flavor is stronger than St. Paulin and other milder *B. linens* ripened cheeses but not as strong as Limburger. Indicative of its flavor, but lack of overpowering

smell, is its reputation as the "married man's Limburger." Its body is firmer than Limburger and its moisture is somewhat less, which accounts at least partially for its milder flavor.

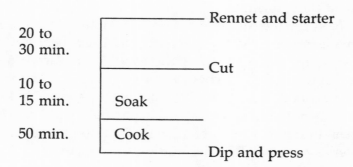

You will need:
>   whole milk (preferably pasteurized)
>   rennet
>   starter
>   rectangular metal molds
>   *B. linens* bacteria (either in the form of
>   another cheese with this bacterial growth
>   on its surface or curing boards that have
>   properly been impregnated)

The milk should be of good quality, free from off-flavors and taints. Whole milk should be used and its bacterial count should be low. If in doubt, pasteurize the milk rather than take a chance as this cheese uses just a small amount of starter. Stabilize the temperature of the milk at 89° or 90° F. Add one tablespoon buttermilk starter for every gallon of milk used. Stir the starter in thoroughly. At this time also add the cheese coloring if desired. Make sure that they are completely mixed and then add the rennet solution, enough to make the milk set up in about 20 minutes. Make sure that the rennet is mixed with 30 to 40 times its own volume of water. Now stir this for two or three minutes in the milk or until you are sure that it is mixed in well.

Let the renneted milk set undisturbed for 25 or 30 minutes until the curd has set up sufficiently to break cleanly over your finger run at an angle under the surface of the curd and then lifted up. You may also just pull the curd away from the sides of the pan and if it retains its shape it will be ready. Now follow the directions in chapter two pertaining to cutting the curd. Cut it into ¼-inch cubes. After cutting, let the curds remain in the whey for ten to fifteen minutes to allow some of the whey to be expelled at that temperature. Agitate during this time to prevent the curds from matting together.

Now start to add heat to the double boiler. This particular cheese is not cooked at a very high temperature. Keep the rise in temperature to one degree every five minutes and heat to a temperature of 96° F. This should take about half an hour, then maintain that temperature for another 20 minutes. During this cooking, agitate slowly and gently to keep the curd from sticking together.

Now dip the curd into the rectangular metal molds. These molds may be made from small metal bread pans that have been perforated with holes to allow the whey to escape. If these molds are placed on a straw or similar mat that will allow the whey to drain away there is no reason for the molds to have a bottom in them. It is perfectly permissible to make molds by merely bending some perforated metal into a square. Allow the cheese to remain in the mold for about 25 to 30 minutes to drain and start to mat under its own weight. Then add a cheese follower to the top of the mold and add a brick to press the cheese.

One note: if you do use a perforated bread pan for a mold, you will have to carefully fill the cheese mold to a point where the pan is larger than the cheese follower since the pan slopes inward toward the bottom. The cheese should be high enough above this point so that as it is compressed, the follower won't be restricted by the sloping sides and its travel impeded at some point where it can't finish pressing the cheese. Leave the cheese in the cheese mold with the weight on it overnight.

After the cheese has been removed from the mold place it in a saltwater solution at about 45° to 50° F. Sprinkle salt on the upper surface that isn't exposed to the brine. Leave the cheese in the brine solution for a day and then remove.

Now the cheese is ready for introduction of the *B. linens*. Any of the methods mentioned at the first of the chapter will do nicely. The easiest method, if you make a lot of cheeses of this type, is to let it ripen on a board to which the *B. linens* have been introduced. If this is not the case, introduce the organism by rubbing it against the surface of a commercially-produced cheese, by using a commercially-prepared culture, or by washing a piece of Limburger or similar cheese in a mild saltwater solution and then rubbing this small amount of inoculated water on the surface of the cheese. It is still necessary to moisten the surface with a mild brine solution and rub the surface of the cheese with it every day. This doesn't introduce the organism—it just makes sure that it is distributed evenly over the surface.

The cheese should be stored in a very moist atmosphere (as close to 95 percent humidity as possible) and at a temperature of between 55° and 65° F. Smear by rubbing the surface with just enough of the mild salt water to moisten it. Moisten the whole surface of the cheese to keep the surface smear as even as possible. If introducing the *B. linens* organism by setting the cheese on edge on wooden boards impregnated with the organism, not only wipe the cheese down every day as just described, but rotate the cheese so that a new edge is exposed to the wooden surface every day. Continue this procedure for approximately two weeks and then paraffin as explained in chapter two. Store the paraffined cheese in a cool (40° to 45° F) place for from one to two months. The higher the temperature the shorter the curing time, but try not to go over 45° F.

Limburger

This unfortunate cheese is the victim of a bad press and over-ripening. The aroma is often described as "strong" by those who like it, but it is called something else entirely by those who have no vested interest in its proliferation. It originated in the province of Luttich in Belgium where the town of Limburger is located. It is the strongest of the *B. linens* bacteria-ripened cheeses. If you can get by the smell, it is a pretty good cheese. Even though its history is marred by many slanders it has had a fairly uneventful existence, except perhaps for the Limburger rebellion during which the Limburger wagon had the misfortune to be parked upwind from the village.

Time	Step	Action
		Rennet and starter
20-30 min.		
		Cut
10 min.	Soak and agitate	
45 min.	Cook	
		Dip
12 hours	Drain and matt	

Note that the manufacture of Limburger is very similar to that of Brick cheese, which is not surprising since the developer of Brick first ran a Limburger factory.

You will need:

      whole milk (good quality, preferably
         pasteurized)
      rennet
      starter
      cheese molds

Stabilize the temperature of the milk at 90° F. Now add one tablespoon of starter for every gallon of milk used. Stir the starter in thoroughly and then add the rennet mixed in 30 to 40 times its volume of water. Mix this in well and let it set for 20 to 30 minutes. Cut the curd into cubes as explained in chapter two. The cubes should be from ⅜-inch to ½-inch in diameter.

The cooking should be done very slowly. First the curd should be agitated for about ten minutes very slowly and gently to help expel the whey. The cooking barely takes place at all. Increase the temperature to 92° F over a period of about ten minutes and then maintain it there for about 30 or 35 minutes. Agitate during this time to prevent the curds from sticking together.

At the end of this time the curd should be dipped into perforated cheese molds. If you have previously made Brick cheese notice that this cheese is softer and has more moisture in it. Usually Limburger is pressed in rectangular cheese molds but there is no law that says this has to be done. The practical reason for rectangular Limburger is that if the cheese is placed on *B. linens*-impregnated boards, it makes it easier to expose a new surface to the bacteria each day as the cheese is rotated. The cheese is allowed to press overnight under its own weight. Since it is a soft cheese, no weight is added to the cheese follower.

The cheese is then floated in a heavy brine solution for two days and loose salt is sprinkled on the upper surface that has not contacted the brine. At the end of that time the cheese is exposed to *B. linens*, which give its characteristic flavor and odor. If the cheese is shaped into its traditional rectangular shape the bacteria can be introduced in the form of *B. linens*-impregnated wooden shelves or curing boards. If not, the bacteria can be introduced by rubbing on some other *B. linens*-ripened cheese surface or wiping the surface of the Limburger with the same moisture that has been used to wipe the surface of an already-ripened cheese. Limburger must be moistened with a small amount of slightly salted water every other day. Make sure that the surface is thoroughly smeared during this time to give the cheese a thick, even coating of *B. linens*. After a week and a half the smearing, though continuing, is done with an even smaller amount of moisture.

So far the discussions have been about the introduction of the *B. linens* to give the cheese its characteristic flavor and aroma, but the conditions under which it is ripened are very important too. The temperature of the storing chamber should be between 40° and 45° F and the humidity should be as high as possible. This high humidity can probably be best maintained in the home by putting the cheese in a plastic bag and then inflating it with the end of the bag tied off so that no air will escape. Excess water should be placed inside the bag and then the cheese placed on a board or rack, whichever is the most convenient. The salting and rubbing every other day should keep down any mold that might appear.

After three weeks in the ripening chamber the cheeses can be taken out. The Limburger can be wrapped in foil or wax paper. It is then usually stored for another two to four weeks to complete the ripening process. If this cheese's strong flavor has discouraged you before, the shorter ripening period will yield a milder product. This mild Limburger is similar to Liederkranz cheese.

Chapter 6

Blue Cheeses

The blue cheeses are another example of originally natural processes that ultimately changed the flavor of some of the existing cheeses. The legend telling of the origin of Roquefort is probably typical of how the blue cheeses came into being. According to legend, a shepherd one day left a cheese made from sheep's milk next to a load of bread. The herd became scattered and he was so busy that not only did he neglect lunch, he even forgot where he had placed it. Some time later he came back through the same area and there was his lunch just where he had left it weeks before. But in the meantime the bread had molded, and this mold had spread to the cheese. Its flavor had changed also. The cheese had ripened and the mold had introduced a delicious new flavor. It seems to have been a common practice at one time to leave a loaf of bread and some cheese together so that this would happen. Even today *Penicillium roqueforti* is cultured by allowing it to grow on bread first.

In this chapter we will be dealing with some of the blue-mold ripened cheeses. In the cheeses discussed in the last chapter the flavor was introduced by *B. linens* growing on the *surface* of the cheese and ripened at a moderate humidity. In this chapter, though there is some surface growth, the mold is introduced and develops in the *interior* of the cheese. Another noticeable difference is the humidity. The mold is encouraged to grow in a humidity condition just short of raining! If you have some means of measuring it, it should be around 95 percent.

Although there are other cheeses that use *P. roqueforti* to give them their distinctive flavors, as well as cheeses that use other molds entirely, this chapter will give directions for just a few, but they're all some of the best. Roquefort is not included, even though it is very popular. The reason is that in order to make it you must use sheep's milk, a very difficult item to find in America. Roquefort cheese was developed in the area of Roquefort, France; an area poor and suitable for grazing only sheep and goats. The sheep used are especially bred for production of milk, not wool, like domestic sheep.

Before making the cheeses in this chapter a mold powder is needed in order to inoculate the cheeses. For this, first buy a small package of some veined blue cheese. Some bread is also needed on which to grow the mold. From the blue cheese, dig out some of the blue-green veins. Spread them on the surface of the bread and put the slice of bread in a dark, damp place. You could, for instance, put the bread on a shallow saucer in a covered cake pan. Sprinkle water on the bottom of the cake pan to promote humidity and keep the bread from drying out. Put the whole thing in a dark, warm place and let the mold grow and cover the whole surface of the bread. When the bread is well covered with mold, remove it from the covered dish and let it dry out. When it is dry, crumble it up into a powder and use this for the mold powder required in the recipes that follow. By the way, you can also purchase mold powders from some of the commercial sources listed in the last chapter.

Gorgonzola

Stracchino di Gorgonzola, or just plain Gorgonzola, this is the blue cheese of Italy. In the latter part of the 9th century this cheese was developed in the beautiful and important Po Valley of Italy. The mold is usually the same as for the other blue cheeses, but it is called *Penicillium glaucum* instead of *Penicillium roqueforti*. Even though the mold is usually the same, the taste certainly isn't. The cheese has a creaminess to it while the better-known Roquefort is saltier, stronger, and has a crumbly texture. It owes its unique texture to the distribution of warm morning curds on the outside and cool curds from the evening before in the center. In order to make this cheese it is necessary to have access to fresh milk.

Evening Milk Curds

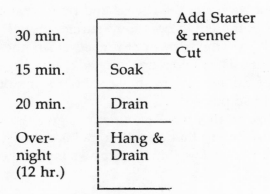

30 min.		Add Starter & rennet — Cut
15 min.	Soak	
20 min.	Drain	
Over-night (12 hr.)	Hang & Drain	

Morning Milk Curds

30 min.		─── Add starter & rennet ─── Cut
15 min.	Soak	
20 min.	Drain	

You will need:
    whole milk
    buttermilk starter
    mold powder

Although now it is generally the procedure to use pasteurized milk, this is not absolutely necessary. The milk, though, should be as free from foreign bacteria as possible to avoid any off-flavors. You will need whole evening milk since the first part of this cheese is made in the evening. Stabilize the evening milk to 86° F and add three tablespoons of buttermilk starter per gallon of milk. Stir the starter in well and then add enough rennet to form a curd in twenty minutes.

Allow the curd to set for half an hour and then cut the curd into ⅜-inch cubes. Try to keep the curds as uniform in size as possible and make sure that the knife cuts all the way to the bottom of the curd. After the curd has been cut, agitate gently for 10 or 15 minutes in a double boiler at 86° F. This will firm and dry out the curd slightly and aid in the expulsion of whey.

The curd can be dipped or, if the cheese is small enough, it might be light enough to pour into a cheesecloth-lined colander or just a cheesecloth spread across the top of a container to catch the whey. Spread the curds out slightly in the colander or on the cheesecloth to allow them to drain more independently of one another and faster. This draining should be done in a moderately warm room. A way to keep the curds warm for a slightly longer period of time, at least during the draining period, is to cover them with a cloth. After the initial draining period of 10 or 15 minutes, the corners of the cheesecloth can be gathered together to make a bag and hung over a sink or some container to catch the whey that will drain during the night. Allow them to mat together in the normal way. The room in which the curds drain overnight should be relatively warm (about 65°F) to encourage the increase of acid.

In the morning the curd should be made just as it was the night before with the exception of the 12-hour draining period. This morning curd should be allowed to mat together but not cool. The matted curd from both batches are then cut up in pieces about one inch square. Make sure to keep the morning and evening curd separated. The regular Gorgonzola cheese

69.550

hoop is about eight or more inches in diameter and about ten inches deep. Of course the quantity of cheese to be made will determine the ultimate size of the cheese mold.

Now comes probably the most important step in the making of Gorgonzola, or at least the step that makes it so unique. The cheese mold is first lined with cheesecloth and then the fresh, warm-morning curd is piled on the bottom and pushed around the sides of the mold. Keep just a little out and save it. Sprinkle a very small amount of the mold powder, made by powdering dry bread on which the mold has been cultured, over the morning curd. Next, the older, evening curd is put in the center, and the remaining fresh, morning curd is placed over the top. It is this unique placement of the curd that gives Gorgonzola its distinctive creamy smoothness. Remove the cheese to a room kept at about 55° F or slightly less.

Lift the ends of the cheesecloth, trim to size if necessary, and fold the ends over the top of the cheese to make a neat bandage. Let it mat together under its own weight for an hour and then it is flipped end for end. Let it stay this way for an hour and then flip it every two hours thereafter for the rest of the day. Continue to turn the cheese several times a day for the next three days. Free the cheese from the cheese mold or hoop and remove the cheesecloth. Rub the cheese surface with table salt. Make sure to rub it on thoroughly. Then, as the initial salting is completed, roll the cheese in the excess salt that has fallen to the shelf. Apply more salt by rubbing it on the surface every other day for the next two weeks. The cheese is now cured for about a month at the same temperature of about 55° F. The humidity should be around 80 percent. Turn the cheese every few days to keep it from becoming deformed and rub it down or remove any growths that appear at this stage. During this stage the cheese is being dried out in preparation for another stage.

Next, the temperature is lowered somewhat (to about 45° F), and the humidity is increased to encourage mold growth. To facilitate this growth, the cheese is punched. In doing this, use a long ice pick or clean piece of wire like a knitting needle that will penetrate all the way through the curd. Push the wire or similar tool through the cheese and work it around just a little to open up an air passage and allow the mold spores to receive air. An 8-inch cheese should have about 15 to 25 holes. Mold should be allowed to grow freely on the cheese surface until well established, at which time it can be controlled by infrequent scrapings. After a month has passed, wash the surface of the cheese and remove its mold. Allow the cheese to ripen about another two months, washing and scraping during this period to keep down the surface growth. It can be used three or four months after being made, but in Italy it is often aged as long as a year. If the cheese is aged for a longer period, try to keep the temperature at 40° F or a degree or two higher.

Stilton is the mildest of the great European blue cheese triumvirate (Stilton, Roquefort and Gorgonzola) and is considered by many to be the finest of the English cheeses. Its flavor is mild and creamy, but the cheese was never made at Stilton; it was just served there! It also appears that the cheese even preceded Mrs. Paulet, the one generally given the credit for this cheese. No matter, the real treat is the cheese, itself, and with a little care you can make a Stilton-type cheese that will be very close to the original.

From listening to the usual descriptions of how Stilton is made, you would think that through some magical process the cheese turns blue. To a certain extent this is correct; the rooms in which Stiltons were cured and made abounded with the *P. roqueforti* mold spores. But to make this cheese at home you will have to add this mold artificially.

The making of Stilton has changed but slightly since its conception. Originally the milk was turned into evening curds which were then mixed with morning curds. The resulting mechanical openings allowed air and mold spores to penetrate the cheese's interior. Now Stilton is made from one batch of milk and the cheese is stabbed with wire needles to allow mold spores and air to penetrate its interior. The cheese is also a single-cream cheese, but in the past it was often made by saving the cream from the previous milking and adding it to the milk used for the cheese.

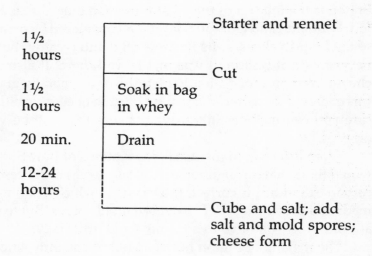

You will need:
- whole milk
- extra cream (optional)
- buttermilk starter
- mold spores

Choose good-quality whole milk. This cheese is made from cow's milk, and if making the double-creamed Stilton it will be necessary to save the cream from the previous milking. Add it to the milk and stir it in. Not only will the added butterfat give a creamier cheese, it will make one that is bigger. Warm the milk to 86° F and add two tablespoons of active buttermilk for every gallon of milk used. Stir the starter in well and add enough rennet to set the milk in an hour and a half. This will be about half the amount normally used for most cheeses.

For the next step it will be necessary to have a room with a temperature between 65° and 70° F. First you will need to make a cloth bag; it can be six or eight layers of cheesecloth or, even better, some cotton cloth. Now cut or break the cheese into thin pieces. If the cheese isn't too large perhaps the easiest way is to simply cut slices out of the curd with a large spoon, then transfer these to the cloth bag in such a way that the whey can run back into the container. When the curd has been transferred to the cloth, its ends are tied together so that it makes a bag. The bag is then dipped into the whey and left there for another hour and a half. At the end of this period the cloth bag is hung up above a container to catch the whey. After about 20 minutes, when the flow of whey has ebbed, the whey is put under pressure to forcibly expel any remaining. One way to do this is to squeeze or twist the bag. Another is to press the whey out using weight. Put a board on a drain board. If no drain board, put something under one end of a board to tilt it toward the sink. Put the curd bag on the board and put another board over the top of the cheese. Then add weight to the upper board.

Leave the cheese under pressure overnight in a warm room. The next day take the cheese out from beneath the weights. It should be firm and able to retain its shape if broken into pieces. If it hasn't achieved this degree of hardness yet let it sit for another six to twelve hours at room temperature until it does. By then the cheese will have developed a ripened taste, but it shouldn't be bitter. Now the curd is broken or cut into chunks an inch or less in diameter. Add a teaspoon of salt for every gallon of milk used and mix it in well. When the salt has been absorbed repeat the procedure twice more so that a total three teaspoons of salt per gallon of milk has been added in three equal portions.

The cheese form consists of a perforated metal can with both ends cut out. The cheeses are usually about eight inches across and of about the same depth.

To get the mold to grow in nice veins inside the cheese first put down a layer of cheese curds. Press them down well and then add a very small sprinkle of mold powder. Be sure to use only a very small amount; it is better to use too little than too much. Now add another layer of curd and another sprinkle of mold powder. Continue until you reach the top of the cheese form. Cover it with a layer of cheese curds, then allow the curds to mat under their own weight for two hours.

Flip the cheese-filled mold every two hours for the first day. Flipping these cheeses is facilitated by slipping a thin piece of metal or stiff paper under the mold to keep the cheese from falling out and another over the top to retain it when the cheese is reversed. Drain the cheese on a cloth-covered draining board. Allow this process to continue for a week, but it is only necessary to turn the cheese over once a day during this period. The mold is pierced for the first time on about the fifth day. Use a piece of wire or a knitting needle to poke about ten holes through the cheese from top to bottom. If the cheese is firm enough at the end of a week it may be taken out of the cheese form and put by itself on the curing shelf. If it is too soft and starts to sag it may be left in the cheese mold until it firms up.

After the first week of curing at room temperature the cheese is moved into a room having a temperature between 55° and 60° F and a high relative humidity (about 90 percent, if you have the means of measuring it). The cheese surface becomes slimy as the mold begins to grow. After the second week of curing and the first week in the high-humidity cooler room, the cheese should again be perforated with knitting-needle-type wires. Make about 20 or 30 holes, depending on the size of the cheese; the needle can be stabbed right through the cheesecloth. After the third week of curing (the second week in the cooler room) the cheesecloth can be removed.

The final stage of curing takes from four months to half a year. The temperature should be held at between 55° and 60° F. and the humidity at around 90 percent. These cheeses will grow mold on their surfaces which should be removed. Clean the cheeses once or twice a week by scraping them down. The perforations in the cheeses will allow air to penetrate to the interior, which will encourage the *P. roqueforti* to grow in veins inside.

When the cheese is finally cured it is susceptible to drying out so to avoid this problem cut out what you want and then cover the cheese with a damp cloth.

Blue Cheese

Domestic Blue Cheese was an attempt to copy the French Roquefort, once microbiology had progressed sufficiently to isolate the organisms responsible for its uniqueness. It is made with cow instead of sheep milk, though, and its flavor and texture are distinctive. The cheese failed as a copy of the French cheese, but became a success in its own right.

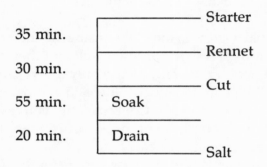

35 min. — Starter
30 min. — Rennet
55 min. — Cut — Soak
20 min. — Drain — Salt

You will need:
    whole milk
    buttermilk starter
    rennet
    mold powder (small amount)

Choose good-quality raw, whole milk. It should have a low bacterial count to help insure that the cheese will be free from off-flavor. Stir any cream that has risen back in carefully. Heat the raw milk and stabilize its temperature at 90° F. Add six tablespoons of buttermilk starter for every gallon of milk used and let the mixture ripen for a period of 35 to 40 minutes at 90° F. At the end of that period add enough rennet to set the milk in about 20 minutes. Make sure that the rennet is mixed with a large volume of lukewarm water. Add the rennet to the milk and mix it in well. Allow the curd to set undisturbed for one-half hour.

After half an hour the curd should be cut into cubes ½-inch or slightly more in diameter as explained in the second chapter. Make sure that the cuts go all the way to the bottom and sides of the container so that the cubes will be as uniform as possible. Allow the curds to remain in the whey for 50 to 60 minutes with occasional agitation to keep the curds from sticking together. Keep the temperature of the curds and whey at 90° F. throughout the cooking procedure.

Either dip the curds and whey out of the cooking container or, if the cheese is small enough, pick up the pan and pour the curds and whey into a colander or a cheesecloth stretched over the top of a pan to catch the whey as it runs off. Remember, the whey can be used for whey cheeses so don't waste it. Allow the whey in the curds to drain 15 or 20 minutes until drained out. To speed draining, it is advisable to shift the curds once or twice to open any whey pockets that might have formed within.

Measure out two teaspoons of salt per gallon of milk originally used and divide it into three equal portions. Sprinkle the three portions evenly across the curd, one at a time, and mix it in completely before the next portion of salt is added. When the salt has been added and has been absorbed by the curd it is time to add the mold. Sprinkle just a tiny bit of the mold powder on the curd. Carefully spread the powder evenly across the curd. If too much is added to the curd or if too much is added in one spot it will make it waxy and hard and very likely ruin the cheese. It is better to add too small an amount than too much. A small pinch should suffice for a cheese made out of two or three gallons of milk. If uneasy about adding the mold at this point, add it to the milk at the same time the starter is added. In this approach add about ⅛ of a teaspoon of the mold powder for every four gallons of milk used. If the mold powder is added to the milk make sure that it is thoroughly mixed by the time the rennet is added.

The next step, that of putting the cheese in cheese forms, should be done in a warm room and at about room temperature. The molds are perforated cheese forms open at both ends. Put the cheese molds on a draining mat or some other area that is porous so the whey can drain through it. Put the curds in the molds and fill to the top. It is important that the molds (or cheese forms, if you will) be small enough so that there will always be enough curd to fill them slightly above the top. The curd will settle somewhat and the full forms will have to be flipped over often so that

the curd will mat evenly under its own weight without breaking up. After the forms have been filled allow the cheese to mat together under its own weight for 20 minutes. Then, by slipping a flat, stiff piece of metal, plastic, or something similar under the cheese form to support the curds in the form and one over the top for same purpose, flip the cheese over. The curd at this point is not very firm and can easily fall out of the cheese form. Flip the cheese every 20 minutes for the first two or three hours after putting in the forms. Keep the room at around 70° F and, after the initial turning to solidify the cheese, let it set in one position overnight.

The next day remove the cheese from the form. It should be firm enough to do so by then. If the cheese sticks in the form remove it by slipping a long, thin-bladed knife around the outside, between the cheese and the curd. After the cheese is out move it to a curing box or room with a temperature of 55° F. For brine, fill a container with water and add salt to it, agitating it until the salt's ability to dissolve slows. Put the cheese in the salt water and sprinkle salt on any surface not exposed to the brine. Turn the cheese daily for four or five days, each time sprinkling salt on the upper surface if it isn't exposed to the brine.

After brining is completed the cheese is removed from the salt water and its surface allowed to dry. Now the cheese must be pierced with a long wire needle, something like a knitting needle. Push the wire all the way through the cheese. This is to allow air to reach the interior of the cheese so that mold will grow there, too. Then put the cheese in a plastic bag with the cheese on a rack or similar device to keep it from touching the plastic. Put some water in the bag to provide the necessary moisture, inflate the bag and tie it off so that the bag won't lose air. Alternatively, the cheese can be put in some other container or room where the humidity can be kept very high (around 95 percent). During its curing, rotate the cheese slightly every day so it won't become deformed by being in one position too long. Every few days the cheese should be wiped down with a clean, moist, rough cloth. Leave it in this environment for three weeks; then carefully scrape and clean the cheese off. The mold will have developed inside the cheese during this time but the flavor won't be fully developed yet. Wrap the cheese in a plastic wrap and store it in a cool place, 40° F. Allow the cheese to mature for three months or until the cheese meets your requirements for flavor.

Blue Cheddar

This Cheddar is one that has been allowed to go blue—that is to say, the cheese is a Cheddar, but *P. roqueforti* is added to it to give it the flavor of the Blue cheeses. It isn't the same as the other Blues, but it is delightful just the same.

Occasionally this cheese happens by accident, but when it does it is considered a fault. It means that blue mold was somehow introduced as a contaminant. For the kitchen cheesemaker it probably means that spores from the Blue cheeses have infected the curing chamber and that it must then be thoroughly cleaned. Save the Blue Cheddar and cherish it, though.

To make a Blue Cheddar on purpose, make a Cheddar according to the directions in the third chapter. The curds will be cheddared and then milled. This will be just before the pressing step. Under normal circumstances the curd is cut into small cubes and then salted. Proceed with this in the usual way. Then add just a little of the same powdered mold spore as used to make the other Blue cheeses in this chapter. There are two ways of doing this. The mold spore can be added to all of the curd and then thoroughly mixed up. The curd will then be added to the cheese form and pressed in the usual manner. Another way, and one that will give a more pronounced vein effect, is to put down a layer of the salted curds. This is followed by sprinkling on a small amount of the mold powder. Then another layer of Cheddar curds is laid down with more mold powder sprinkled on top of it. This is repeated, making each layer of curds approximately one to two inches thick, until the cheese mold is filled.

After the curds are put in the cheese form the cheese is pressed in the normal manner. After pressing, the cheese must be needled to allow air to enter its interior so the mold can grow more easily. A stiff wire the size of a knitting needle is ideal. Push the wire completely through the cheese. The curd at this point is elastic and can close back over the hole if the wire is too small. A cylindrical cheese six inches in diameter should probably be pierced at least a dozen times. Allow the cheese to cure normally. It is not unusual to get a blue surface growth. This can be encouraged for a week or two and then be scraped off. By this time the mold should be well established inside. It will be blue within three or four weeks after the cheese was made, and until that happens the cheese should be kept perhaps a little more moist than one would normally keep a Cheddar. The reason for this is that mold needs a high moisture content; the cheese shouldn't be allowed to dry out or crack. After the mold is well established the cheese should be cleaned off to remove any surface growth and then paraffined in the usual way. Store it in a cool place at around 50° F. This is an unusual and personal cheese so it should be ripened until it suits your taste.

Gex

This is a Blue cheese whose manufacture is reminiscent of the primitive goat milk cheeses. It is set without a starter by just adding rennet while the milk is still warm from the cow. It follows that if unable to get this ingredient, making Gex will not be a realistic project for some home cheesemakers.

```
                              ┌──────────────── Rennet
       2 hours                │
                              ├──────────────── Break curd
       15 min.                │
                              │
       45 to         Drain    │
       60 min.                │
                              ├──────────────── First salting
       24 hours      Press    │
                              └──────────────── Second salting
```

You will need:

        whole milk (as fresh as possible)

        rennet (for coagulating the milk)

        P. roqueforti (to give it its characteristic flavor)

Bring the milk in directly from milking while it is still as warm as possible. Mix slightly less rennet than you normally would—use an amount of water equal to 30 or 40 times the volume of the rennet. Rather than use cool water for this mix, put the rennet in water that is warm, but not over 102° F, the temperature at which rennet starts to break down. Mix the rennet in well and leave it in a warm spot free from jarring for the two-hour coagulating period.

At this stage a cheese is normally cut into cubes, but with Gex there is a slight difference; instead of cutting the curd into cubes, break the curd up. After the initial breaking, stir the curd with something that will further reduce the size of the curds such as a pastry whisk. After the curd has been broken up into small pieces agitate for a period of ten to fifteen minutes, to keep the curd from matting together.

Now pour the curds and whey into several thicknesses of cheesecloth to avoid losing the very small pieces of curd. Be sure to save the whey from this cheese. Because of the manner in which the curd is cut, this whey is much richer in butterfat than that of many other cheeses. After the whey has been drained, salt the curd in the usual way. Add one teaspoon of salt per gallon of milk used and mix it in well. Then add another teaspoon of salt per gallon and mix it in well, also.

When the salt has been mixed in and absorbed by the cheese put the curd in the cheese mold or form. Traditionally, these are about a foot in diameter and about half that deep, but Gex can be made in any size desired. As in most cases, though, the larger cheeses are better flavored than the small ones. Put the cheese follower on the top of the curd and add weight. Allow the cheese to set in the press at cool room temperature and with a moderate amount of weight for a day. During the pressing, turn the cheese about every four hours.

After one day in the press the cheese can be removed from the mold. The exterior of the cheese is salted by rubbing it with some fine salt. The cheese is then moved to a room of relatively high humidity (about 90%) and where the temperature is between 45° and 50° F. The cheese will take three to four months to ripen. The mold is allowed to ripen only on the surface of the cheese, much as with a Coon cheese. This cheese can be ripened in the same chamber with a Blue cheese with good results because the Gex will pick up spores from the other cheese. If there are no naturally occurring spores in the curing chamber they can be introduced by rubbing a small amount of blue mold powder (described at the beginning of this chapter) on its surface. The mold should be allowed to grow until it covers the whole surface. Too luxuriant a growth can be restrained by occasional washings with salt water, but it probably won't be necessary.

Chapter 7

Camembert

Camembert is another cheese that owes its characteristic flavor to a mold. The mold in this case is white instead of blue and comes to us by accident, probably out of the 13th century. Camembert, itself, didn't come into existence until 1791 when it was developed by Marie Fontain. It is said that Napoleon named the cheese when he found that it had no name. The cheese received a good press and is often called the queen of cheeses.

There are other cheeses that use *P. camemberti* but Camembert is one of the best. The other contender for the crown of best *P. camemberti*-ripened cheeses and, maybe for the best of all cheeses, is Brie. In addition to *P. camemberti*, Brie is surface-ripened by *B. linens*, but the extreme difficulty of its manufacture takes it beyond the realm of this book. Camembert is also very difficult but with some persistence it is possible to make a first-quality cheese. The cheese forms a crust covered with white whiskers of mold while the inside is creamy and smooth.

Before proceeding, some form of *P. camemberti* will be needed. You may send off to one of the sources in the very last chapter of this book and buy it from them; or, if there is a cheese shop in the vicinity, it may be better to simply buy a Camembert from them. If you do the latter, shave off a portion of the outer surface of the cheese crust. Mash and dissolve as much of this as possible in a couple of cups of sterile water. The water should be sterilized by boiling rather than by adding chemicals since this might inhibit the growth of the mold. When the outer surface has been mashed and dissolved in the water, strain off the solid portions of the cheese that remain. Once the inoculating fluid has been prepared, there are two ways of adding the mold to the cheese. It is permissible to add the mold solution to the milk, but better results are obtained by spraying the aqueous solution of mold spores on the cheese with an atomizer.

Another important thing is to have the right size cheese mold or form. It should be a perforated metal band four and a half inches in diameter and one inch deep. The size of the mold and the relation of the width to the depth makes a difference with this cheese.

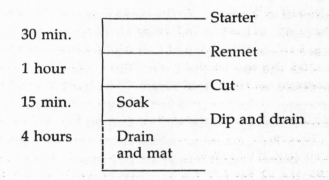

You will need:
        whole milk
        starter
        rennet
        special cheese form
        aqueous solution of *P. camemberti*

The milk should be of good quality and it must also be whole. Because it is a difficult cheese and one that takes more than the average amount of time and trouble to make, the milk should also be pasteurized if there is any doubt about its bacterial count. To do this, heat the milk to 162° F for half a minute. Cool the milk down to 90° F and stabilize its temperature at that point. Now add five tablespoons of active buttermilk for every gallon of milk used. Mix the starter in thoroughly, cover and, keeping the temperature still at 90° F, let it stand for 30 minutes. At the end of that time mix the rennet in some cool water and add to the milk. Stir it in well and let it stand undisturbed for one hour. Enough rennet should be added to the milk to make it set up in 20 to 25 minutes. The extra time is to allow the curd to set up very firmly.

Because the curd is very firm you will have to use a very sharp knife to cut it. The curd is cut into cubes between ½-inch and ⅝-inch in diameter. Make certain that the cuts extend all the way to the bottom and sides of the cooking container and that the angle cuts are even and carefully spaced.

In order to achieve its soft, creamy characteristics, the cooking step is omitted. A 15-minute soak period is required, however, to firm the individual curds somewhat and help in the expulsion of whey. Keep the temperature at 90° F. At the end of 15 minutes the curd and whey should be put into the molds. Several methods are used to put the cheese in the molds but the easiest for the home cheesemaker is to ladle the curds and whey out of the cooking container using a large ladle or a small saucepan. The curd should be ladled directly into the cheese molds. The molds should be placed on top of draining mats. There are differences of opinion whether to dip the curds into the mold with as little breaking as possible or whether to funnel them into the molds. The latter results in a good deal of breaking. Both methods can result in a good final product if the other steps are adhered to, however, so the method is a matter of personal perference. Fill the molds to the top and, once filled, add no more curds to the cheese. The curds should be heaped just slightly to allow the cheese to settle to even with the top of the form. The curds should be drained at room temperature for about four hours. The object of this long draining period without any weight or pressure on the curds is to allow them time to mat together naturally. At the end of that period put a piece of metal or stiff paper over the top and another beneath and quickly flip the mold over. Allow it to mat together now for two hours in the inverted position and then flip it back over. Make sure to remove the stiff paper from beneath so it can continue to drain. Now repeat the flipping process three times at hourly intervals to further help compact the curd.

So far the manufacture of this cheese is very similar to the other mold-ripened cheeses. For Camembert cheese, though, the procedure is to use the white mold *P. camemberti*. If the mold culture wasn't added to the milk during the ripening period it should be put on the cheese now. Remove the mold that was suspended in sterile water and put it in a clean atomizer or similar device and spray it on the surface of the cheese. The spray should lightly cover the cheese; it should not be put on so thick that it begins to drip. The surface should be just lightly dampened. Cover one side of the cheese, then let it dry. After the first side is dry the cheese should be turned over and the other side inoculated by spray.

The cheese should be sufficiently firm at this point to remove from the cheese mold. Slip a thin, flexible-bladed knife between the edge of the cheese and the mold and slip it around the outside to loosen it. Allow it to set for a few hours in a warm room to let the mold-impregnated water on the surface of the cheese dry and firm the cheese up. Now take a pan of coarse salt and dip half the cheese in it, much the same as you would dip the cheese in paraffin to wax it. Take the cheese out and, by holding onto the salted portion, dip the other half into the salt. Shake off any excess granules and move to the curing room.

So far, making this cheese hasn't been overly difficult. The ripening is the most difficult part of the process. For the first three weeks the cheese should be held at approximately 85 percent humidity or perhaps just slightly higher. The temperature should be adjusted to as close to 55° F as possible. Keep the cheese on a small-mesh wire screen to assure proper ventilation until whiskers of white mold begin to appear, then turn the cheese over. This white mold growth is desirable but it can cause a problem if it becomes prolific too soon. During this time if the temperature and humidity is controlled precisely the cheese will dry out slightly as the ripening progresses.

The final stage of curing is carried on with a temperature of 50° F or perhaps just slightly less. The cheese is often ripened for one to two weeks in this last stage, but it can vary. If the mold fails to grow well or if the crust cracks and dries, increase the humidity slightly.

This last stage is a ticklish one so a few more things should be said about it. If a French Camembert mold was used instead of a domestic one, the surface characteristics are apt to be entirely different. It seems that it has a mixed surface growth. Such a cheese will then ripen to a darkish white, then spots of yellow may appear, and finally the surface will become a sort of reddish-brown. When this last stage is reached and the surface is also slightly sticky, it should be ready to eat. If the cheese was inoculated with only *P. camemberti*, the surface will be white and the interior will be yellow. Remove any growths of blue-green surface mold that might appear. If opened when just right there will be just a hint of white in the core, but the rest of the interior will have a soft, creamy texture. The cheese should not have an ammonia smell. If it does have, it means that it is over-ripe.

Chapter **8**

The Italian Cheeses

The determining factor for whether a cheese is Italian or not depends on where it really originated. Some of these cheeses naturally fall into other categories: For instance, Gorgonzola, while Italian, is also blue. This chapter includes some of the better-known Italian cheeses that don't quite fit in the chapters devoted to special categories.

Apart from their place of origin, the Italian cheeses, as a general rule, differ from other cheeses by using a yogurt starter rather than a lactic-type starter such as cultured buttermilk. The organisms in yogurt are heat-loving and as a result the cheeses that use them are generally cooked and incubated at a higher temperature than would normally be the case with other starters.

Mozzarella

This is one of the cheeses from southern Italy. Originally it was made from the milk of the water buffalo which is very high in fat content (one of the things contributing to its uniqueness). Now it is made from cow's milk. Bear in mind that the lower the fat content the harder the cheese and the less pronounced will be the characteristic bland, nutty flavor. Another characteristic of this cheese is its elasticity. It contains no salt and its chief use is in pizzas or other Italian-type cooking. The cheeses are traditionally about half a pound.

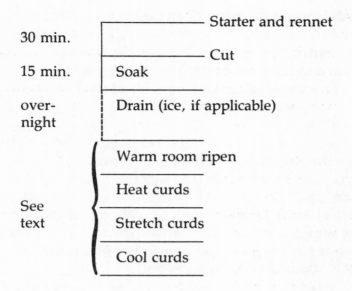

30 min.	Starter and rennet
	Cut
15 min.	Soak
over-night	Drain (ice, if applicable)
See text	Warm room ripen
	Heat curds
	Stretch curds
	Cool curds

In addition to the regular equipment and ingredients you will need:
>   yogurt starter
>   lactic starter or buttermilk
>   ice

Before beginning the cheese, the starter will have to be prepared. If preferred, Mozzarella can be made with a regular lactic starter, but when you do this, however, it involves the extra step of icing. If you don't mind making up cultures or have some fresh yogurt on hand you can make a combination starter that avoids that extra step. Simply add seven tablespoons buttermilk and six tablespoons of active yogurt for every two gallons of milk. Mix it in thoroughly. If you'd like the option of icing the curd, use six tablespoons of buttermilk starter for every gallon of milk used.

Generally whole milk is standardized at three percent fat for this cheese. Pasteurize whole milk by the short-hold method. Lower the temperature to 90° F. Add no color. This cheese is traditionally white.

When the temperature has been stabilized at 90° F add the starter chosen. Mix it in thoroughly, then immediately add the rennet solution. No ripening time is needed by Mozzarella before being set.

Let the curd harden for between 20 minutes and half an hour. It will be ready when the curd breaks cleanly over a clean finger or a dairy thermometer. Now cut in the regular manner as explained in the second chapter. Cut into squares slightly larger than ½-inch. Try to keep the cubes of curd as even as possible. Make sure that the cuts extend all the way to the bottom of the container to eliminate any abnormally large pieces.

Next comes the cooking, but here is the surprise; don't! Just leave the curds in the warm whey. Keep the temperature at 90° F. The curds will be somewhat fragile because they won't be heat-firmed so better results are obtained by gentle agitation with a well-washed hand. Agitate just enough to keep the curds from matting together.

Line the colander with a couple of layers of cheesecloth and pour in the curds and whey. Allow the curd to mat together at this point. Now, while it is still in the colander, rinse in cold tap water and then immerse in cold water for 15 minutes. If you're especially fond of this cheese and it is a big batch, the matted curd should be cut into pieces no larger than four or five inches square. This is so that the blocks or chunks of curd can cool more rapidly in the cold water. Then remove and hang up in the cheese-cloth to drain. Let them drain for a few moments until the extensive flow has stopped, maybe three or four minutes, and then allow to continue draining in a cool room or refrigerator. The temperature should be about 40° F. Allow it to drain overnight.

If lactic starter was used instead of the combination starter there is an extra step to perform at this point. Put the curd bundles on an antiseptic drain board. Immediately cover with crushed ice and let the cheese drain overnight. This is to slow the ripening rate of the curds and prevent them from becoming too ripe too fast.

Now comes the most difficult part of making this cheese. After allowing the cheese to drain overnight, start to ripen the cheese. This ripening has already begun, of course, when the cheese was put in the cheesecloth, but thus far the process has been very slow. In order to hurry it up, take it out of the cool draining area and allow it to warm to room temperature.

It will be ready for the next step when the pH has decreased to about 5.3. Since few care to take the time and trouble to bother with exact acidity in kitchen cheesemaking, here is another method of telling exactly when to begin the next step. Proceed as follows—cut off a small slice of cheese and slice it into ½-inch cubes. Fill a small sauce pan, or similar container with water and heat to 165° F. Put in three cubes of cheese and agitate them with a slotted spoon for about five minutes. Remove them from the water and mold them together as would be done with modeling clay. Dunk in the hot water for another minute or so, so that the curd will warm up again. Remove from the water with the slotted spoon and gently try to pull apart. Repeat this process several times. If the curd breaks or tears off into small sections and the water becomes cloudy it means that the curd is under-ripe. It is ready when a curd sample pulls into a long rope and can be molded back together again. At this point the water will become only slightly cloudy and the stretched curd will have a glossy surface.

Processing is the next step and is quite similar to the stretch test. Dice the cheese into small cubes and put them in a pan. Now heat some water to about 170° F and pour it over the curds; pour in enough so that it covers the curds by about two inches. Keep a thermometer in the water and monitor the temperature while agitating the curd with a slotted spoon. Stabilize the temperature at 135° F; do not let it exceed this. Do not add heat directly but rather add either hot or cold water to stabilize the temperature. Now in go the clean hands, to pull, stretch and knead until the cheese becomes plastic. It should become stretchy and pull into long strings, just as it did in the stretch test. It is somewhat like saltwater taffy. Shape it into balls about half a pound in weight. These may be wrapped in cheesecloth or else dipped in hot water to get a glossy surface. In either case, after everything else is done, dip the cheese blocks in cool salt water for four or five hours to cool them off and give them just a hint of salt. Store in a cool place under 40° F. This is an excellent cheese to freeze and it may be stored in the deep freeze or freezing compartment of the refrigerator until needed.

Romano

Romano is a popular, aromatic, hard-grating cheese from Italy. It can be made from sheep, goat or cow milk (Pecorino Romano, Caprino Romano and Vacchino Romano). From an Italian's point of view, probably most of the cheeses you will be turning out will be Romanellos, or little Romanos, but the only difference is in size. This is a good one to use as a table cheese when aged about a half a year. When older it becomes an exceptional grating cheese.

```
                                  ┌─────── Starter
           10 min.                │
                                  ├─────── Rennet
           30 min.                │
                                  ├─────── Cut
           1 hour                 │
           15 min.        Cook    │
                                  ├─────── Drain
           20 min.                │
                                  └─────── Salt
```

You will need:
    raw milk
    yogurt starter
    rennet

The milk should be a good-quality raw milk that is partially skimmed. The fat is usually slightly more than two percent. Stabilize the milk at 90° F, then add five tablespoons of yogurt that has been made recently to assure proper starter activity. Stir the starter in thoroughly and then let it set for about ten minutes at the ripening temperature of 90° F. Now add the rennet. Add enough so that it will form a curd in 20 to 25 minutes. Let the renneted milk set for half an hour after the rennet has been added.

Now with a sharp knife cut the curd vertically into strips 1/8-inch to 3/16-inch wide. Rotate the container of coagulated milk 90 degrees and again cut the curd into strips the same size. The curd will now be approximately ¼-inch and will reach all the way to the bottom. Allow the curd to remain in the whey for about 15 minutes with only a small amount of agitation to begin to expel the whey and firm the curd up somewhat. After 15 minutes stir what is left of the long strips of curd briskly with a pastry whisk to cut the curd into the small rice-kernel size pieces that are needed for this cheese. Make sure that the pastry whisk is passed all the way to the bottom and close around the sides to break up all the pieces.

Now begin to increase the heat slowly. The temperature of the curds and whey in the inner portion of the double boiler should only rise at the rate of about one degree every two minutes. Maintain this increase in temperature for 45 minutes and until the heat of the curds and whey reaches 115° F. Continue to slowly agitate the curds all during this cooking period. At the end of this heat increase stabilize the temperature at 115° F and continue to agitate until the curds are firm. The only real way to tell when to dip the curds is by developing a feel for this cheese. This feel is easily acquired, though. The curd should be firm enough to retain its shape when a handful is squeezed together. This should be about an hour and 15 minutes after the cooking has started. After the cooking temperature has been reached it is permissible to dip out some of the whey to concentrate the curd in the bottom of the cooking container. If making a full-size Romano this step is almost unavoidable, but since this is a partially skimmed-milk cheese—meaning that the volume of cheese obtained from a certain quantity of milk will be relatively small compared to a whole milk cheese—it will be very handy even with a Romanello.

Dip or pour the remaining curds and whey into a colander lined with cheesecloth. Allow the curds to drain and speed up the process, tugging on one corner of the cheesecloth every once in a while. This will shift the position of the curd slightly and allow any pockets of whey that have been trapped inside to be opened up to allow the whey to drain more easily. Allow to drain 15 or 20 minutes. Let the curd retain as much of the heat as you can. Do this by covering the curd with clean cloth or by setting the colander in the inner cooking kettle and putting a lid or covering over it. After draining, spread the curd out on a board or in a large bowl and add one teaspoon of salt for every gallon of milk used. Mix in well and add another teaspoon for every gallon of milk and mix it in well. Repeat a third time.

Line the cheese hoop or cheese mold with cheesecloth and then put the curd into the molds. Shake the sides and push the curd around slightly so that it flows into the corners of the mold. Cut the cheesecloth if necessary and bandage it over the top so that it forms a neat bandage. Put the cheese follower on top of the curd and apply weight. Press for an hour with a good amount of weight (15 or 20 pounds). At the end of that time take the cheese out of the mold, turn it over and put the follower on what was the bottom of the cheese. Press again for an hour and repeat the process another three or four times. When evening comes, take the cheesecloth off and leave the cheese in the press at room temperature. The next day take the cheese out of the cheese press and put it in a salt solution. Many of the salt solutions that are used for cheeses are saturated solutions—meaning that they can hold no more salt under normal conditions. But this salt solution isn't quite saturated. The way to achieve the right solution is to dissolve all the salt possible in a container of water at between 50° and 60° F. Then add a cup of water for every quart of salt water. Put the cheese in the salt water and cover the top of the container with plastic wrap to keep the water from evaporating. For the next two months turn the cheese over in the brine daily and reseal the plastic wrap over the top of the container to keep the water from evaporating. The cheese in the salt water should be kept at about 50° to perhaps 55° F for this period.

At the end of the two month period the cheese can be removed from the brine and dried off. Now it goes into the final phase of curing which will last up to a year. Keep it in a fairly moist atmosphere, but one not as humid as that used for the mold-ripened cheeses, to keep it from splitting. Try to keep the temperature at around 55° F. During the final ripening period turn and check the cheese two to three times a week. If any mold growing on the surface is detected, simply scrape it off. If mold becomes a

problem it probably means that the humidity is too high. Rubbing shortening or some other form of edible oil on the surface will help keep mold from growing and keep the surface of the cheese from cracking and drying out.

Parmesan

Parmesan is one of the almost immortal cheeses as far as cheese longevity is concerned. The name actually refers to a group of very closely related cheeses in Italy. Like most Italian cheeses it uses one of the special heat-loving cultures instead of the standard ones used in most other cheeses. It can be eaten while young, but is most popular when it has been allowed to mature. It takes a lot of willpower not to nibble on a Parmesan until it becomes a Stravecchione (a four-year-old Parmesan). Perhaps the most sincere compliment that can be paid to this cheese is simply to say that it gets nibbled up before anyone can tell how old it could really become!

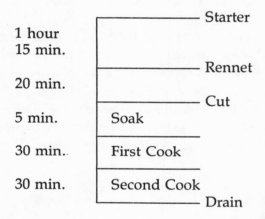

You will need:
      partially skimmed milk
      active yogurt starter
      rennet
      hot iron (for test)

The milk should be partially skimmed but the exact amount of milk fat removed depends on the exact type of Parmesan being made. The less the fat content the smaller the cheese and the harder it will be. In the United States a cheese of acceptable quality, flavor and hardness is made from milk in which the fat level has been regulated to slightly under two percent. The milk used is usually pasteurized, but traditionally in Italy the evening milk is allowed to ripen slightly, as in the case of Stirred-curd, to develop a certain amount of acidity. The temperature of the milk should be stabilized at 95° F and then three tablespoons of yogurt starter for every gallon of milk used should be added. If raw milk has been allowed to ripen overnight, the milk will already have a certain amount of acidity and after the starter has been allowed to mix in the milk well the rennet may be added. If the milk has been pasteurized or has not been allowed to ripen, it is preferable to let it ripen at the holding temperature of 95° F for an hour to an hour and 15 minutes. The rennet should be added and thoroughly mixed in the inoculated milk. The milk should set for about 20 minutes or slightly less. In contrast to making other cheeses, it is important that the milk should *not* be allowed to coagulate until it will break cleanly over a finger pushed at an angle under the curd and then lifted up, as in the usual case. Instead, the curd should be slightly less firm than that. At this point it will have more of a jellylike consistency than normal for most cheeses. Part of the reason for this is that the curd must be cut in very small strips and a very firm curd is almost impossible to cut into strips as small as ⅛-inch. The curd is cut into strips ⅛-inch in diameter and then the pan of curd is rotated 90 degrees and the procedure repeated. Make the cuts directly up and down. When this has been done the curd will be in strips ⅛-inch by ⅛-inch that extend to the pan bottom. Allow the curd to stand undisturbed for five or ten minutes to keep fat loss at a minimum, then begin to stir gently with your hand. As the curd firms the temperature should be raised ten or twelve degrees. Since a heat-loving starter is used and the curd is cut very small, it allows raising the temperature quite rapidly. The temperature may be stepped up as rapidly as one degree a minute. After the curds and whey have been brought up to 105° to 108° F, hold them at that temperature for 15 to 20 minutes. The whole period—from starting the temperature increase to the end of the 15 minute holding period—should take about half an hour.

As the initial half-hour of cooking progresses the curd should be stirred more vigorously. This stirring will also break the long strings of curd into smaller lengths. As the curd firms even more, swish a pastry whisk through it. This will break up the curd into small grain-size particles.

At the end of the 15 or 20 minute holding period at 105° F the curd should be heated to the still higher temperature of 125° F. This will necessitate a 20 degree increase in 35 minutes. The exact time to draw the whey is largely a matter of feel. The curd should be firm but still it should mat together slightly when you wad a handful of it together. Because it is so difficult to explain just what the curd will feel like when it is ready and the time required to reach this stage can vary unexpectedly, it is a good idea to check the acidity of this cheese. Let the curd settle to the bottom and rest there until the acidity of the whey is .19 or slightly less. An alternative to one of the chemical tests for acidity is the "hot iron test," which will do almost as well. The greater the acidity the longer the threads of cheese that will string out from a hot iron pressed against it and then pulled away. Heat a very clean spike or large nail or a small piece of pipe and press it against the cheese. The metal should be hot enough to just melt the cheese. Grab a handful of cheese curds and squeeze out as much whey as possible. Touch the hot metal to the cheese, then draw it away. The threads of cheese stretching between the cheese and the hot metal should be just a tiny bit shorter than ⅛-inch long.

As the acidity increases, dip off part of the whey to facilitate the next step, but the whey shouldn't be drained below the tops of the curds. When the curds have reached the proper consistency, line the colander with cheesecloth and pour or ladle the remaining curds and whey into it. Allow the curds to drain for about 15 minutes. Draining can be speeded up somewhat by holding the four corners of the cheesecloth and tying them together to form a bag. Then, by lifting up one side and then the other, the curds will be shifted and any pockets of whey will open to drain out.

After the draining period the curds can be poured into a cheese form lined with cheesecloth. Shake the mold slightly to settle the curd and put on a draining mat. Fold the cheesecloth over so that it makes a neat bandage, and place it in a cheese press. Put the cheese follower on top, add weight and let it set for an hour. After that interval turn the cheese over. Put the follower on the side that is now up and press for another hour. Turn the third time, but this time let it set overnight and put quite a bit of pressure on it from the cheese press—20 to 30 pounds is about right. All of this can be done at room temperature.

Next the cheese should be moved to the curing room or wherever there is a temperature of about 50° F. Prepare a container of salt solution with as much salt in it as will dissolve. As with all the brine-salted cheeses, the container holding the salt water should not be iron or something that will be corroded by the salt water. Stir in salt until it will hold no more. Remove the cheesecloth and put the cheese in the brine. Salt any exposed upper surface of the cheese. Hold in the salt water and turn daily for two weeks, always salting any exposed upper surface. If the cheese is a very large one, increase the salting period by several days. After two weeks take the cheese out of the salt water and allow to dry for a week. Then it is put in the curing room or chamber where the temperature is around 50° F and humidity is about 80 percent. Turn the cheese once or twice a week during the curing period and be on the lookout for soft spots, usually occurring where the cheese has been lying on the curing shelf. The cheese is not paraffined, but rubbed with oil to prevent mold growth.

How long to mature Parmesan is up to you, but plan on at least eight months. A Vecchio is an old Parmesan (two years), a Stravecchio is a cheese three years old, and Stravecchione is one that has survived for four years.

Chapter 9

Swiss Cheese

Swiss cheese has been made in the Emmental Valley of Switzerland since probably the middle 1400s. Its taste and characteristics are so well-known that there is little left to be said, but a few things should be mentioned about making it, however. While it isn't beyond the capabilities of the home cheesemaker, it is one of the more difficult cheeses to make. It requires a yogurt, instead of a buttermilk starter. To make good Swiss cheese, a proper one to one ratio should be maintained in the yogurt starter. In addition to that, an extra organism, *Propionibacterium shermanii*, is required to form propionic acid which is responsible for forming the eyes as well as giving the cheese its unique flavor. None of these problems are insurmountable, however, and probably worth the extra trouble to any-one who really loves this cheese.

30 min		Starter and rennet
30-40 min.	Soak	Cut
1 hour 15 min.	Cook	
		Dip curds

You will need:
- good quality raw milk
- special starter
- wire pastry whisk
- rennet
- cheese hoop or form

A first concern should be the starter. You will have to decide well in advance in order to obtain the *Propionibacterium shermanii*. It may be ordered from one of the supply houses listed in the last chapter. Yogurt made up of one part *S. thermophilus* to one part *L. bulgaricus* is also needed. Unfortunately, most yogurt cultures don't list the culture proportions on the label, though a few years from now they may. Another problem is that over a period of time one or the other of the cultures in a combination culture gain the upper hand and grow faster, crowding out the other bacteria.

Obtain a new start of yogurt, perhaps a freeze-dried start from one of the supply houses. Make it up into an active culture by adding it to milk. Now mix up the special *P. shermanii* that was obtained as a special culture. A third flask or bottle is needed in which to mix the combination culture. The combination will be six parts *S. thermophilus*, six parts *L. bulgaricus* and one part *P. shermanii*. It will therefore be necessary to add 12 teaspoons yogurt culture to one teaspoon *P. shermanii* culture. Mix it up well just before beginning to make the cheese to insure having a fresh starter.

Now collect the milk. As for all quality cheeses, a good-quality milk is needed to begin with. Almost all Swiss cheese (or Emmental, if you prefer) is made from raw milk. Just make sure it is free from off-flavors and that it is clean. Put the milk in the double boiler and stabilize the temperature at 95° F. Now add the special culture prepared beforehand at the rate of one tablespoon per gallon of milk. Notice that the initial heat of 95° F is higher than that of most cheeses. The *S. thermophilus* (meaning heat-loving) will start to produce acidity at this temperature. Stir the starter in well and then immediately add enough rennet to coagulate the milk in about 20 minutes. Make sure it is mixed in an adequate amount of water. Stir the rennet in thoroughly and then let the curd set without disturbing the container. No ripening period is required before the rennet is added.

Let the curd set for about half an hour. By this time the curd should be ready to cut, but this will be done somewhat differently than with most cheeses. In this case small cubes aren't small enough; the curd will have to be the size of small grains. A good way to achieve this in the kitchen is to first cut the curd vertically into ⅛-inch strips. Then, keeping the knife straight up and down, cut same-sized strips at a 90 degree angle so that from above the curd appears to be cut into tiny ⅛-inch squares but, in reality, they will be small, very long rectangles—⅛-inch by ⅛-inch—and extending all the way to the bottom. Make no diagonal cuts! Now, using the pastry whisk, stir the curd around the container in sweeping motions. Make sure it passes through all levels of the curd. The object is to break all those long strips of curd into small pieces, rather like grain. Occasionally bring up curd from the bottom and sides to see how well they are breaking up. Allow about 15 minutes for this stage. During the cutting, try to keep the temperature stabilized at 95° F.

Now the cooking begins, but don't raise the temperature for 30 to 40 minutes. This stage is called "foreworking" and it varies, depending on how quickly the milk ripens. It should be ready when it feels fairly firm. Keeping the whey at 95° F, agitate the curd. After half an hour, start increasing the temperature by one degree a minute. This is faster than normal, but the curd is very small and it has already been subjected to cooking temperatures for a half an hour or more. After it has reached a temperature of 125° F, stabilize the temperature and continue to cook and slowly agitate for about 45 minutes.

The test of when the cooking is completed is to wad up a few curds together, then break the wad apart or rub it between your palms. If it readily breaks apart into separate pieces again, and if it is firm and crumbly, it is ready.

Now let the curd settle for a few minutes and dip some of the whey off. This will concentrate the curds more and make the dipping easier. Proceed to dip, using a sieve or a colander with small holes. One of the best dippers is a hoop, very much like a landing net with cheesecloth stretched across it. Dip the curd into a cheesecloth suspended across the top of a container or sink to catch the dripping whey. When the curds have been dipped out of the whey, hold the four corners so that it makes a big bag. Now dip the bag of curds back into the whey. Lift them back out and place the whole bag into the cheese hoop. This redipping will make the curd fit the cheese hoop better and reduce the likelihood of voids or cracks in the cheese. Now don't just drop the cheese in the hoop, rather twist the top around several times so that the curd is held in a tight-fitting bag. Using a hand, press the cheese gently into the hoop. As it spreads in the hoop and fills it, loosen the top of the bag to allow it to flow into the corners and edges of the hoop. When it is all worked into place push three or four straight pins under the edge of the hoop or mold. This will allow the whey to drain beneath the hoop. Untwist the top of the cheesecloth, straighten and fold smoothly over the top.

Put the cheese follower on top of the curd and apply pressure, but do so for only about five minutes. Remove the weight and unfasten the cheese hoop or push out of the mold, whichever the case. Take the cheese out and the cheesecloth off. Replace the cheesecloth and put a disk of burlap or similar clean heavy cloth on the top and bottom. This keeps the cheesecloth from being pushed permanently into the cheese. Put back into the cheese mold or hoop and press using light weights. Keep the cheese in the press for about three hours, then take it out. Remove the heavy cloth disks, rinse them in salt water, wring them out well and then replace them on the cheese. Put the cheese back in the mold or cheese hoop and put in the press again under light pressure for another three hours. Repeat the above process once more, but this time let the cheese remain in the press under light weight overnight.

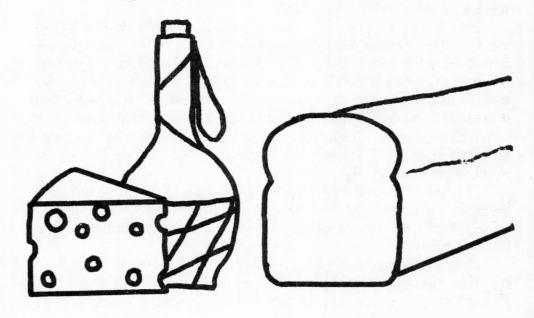

Put some water in a container big enough for the cheese to float in. Add salt and agitate until there are salt crystals in the bottom that will not dissolve. (Do not use a container that will be corroded by the salt!) Put the container in the area used as a curing chamber. The temperature should be 45° to 50° F. Float the cheese in this brine and sprinkle salt on the upper surface that isn't exposed to the salt water. The next day turn the cheese over and again sprinkle salt on the top.

The day after that remove the cheese from the brine and put it on a clean board in an area five to ten degrees warmer than when it was in brine. That means 50° to 55° F or perhaps a little more. The atmosphere should be very moist here also (around 90 percent humidity). Now, daily for a week and a half, the board should be wiped off and dried. The cheese should be wiped off with a clean, salt-soaked cloth and then turned over. After this has been done the surface of the cheese should be given a final salting. Rub the surface thoroughly with table salt.

Now that the salt has been introduced to the cheese the temperature is increased to about 70° F and the humidity can be lowered somewhat, though it should still be moist. Continue to wipe the cheese with clean salt water and turn and salt the surface of the cheese. This only needs to be done twice weekly now, but it should be continued for between a month and a month and a half. As this stage continues the rind color will deepen and the characteristic eye or holes will begin to form. This will cause the cheese to puff up and become rounder and fatter than its original shape.

By now the cheese should be ready for final curing. It should be stored in a place just warm enough to develop and mature its flavor. Keep the temperature between 40° and 45° F. Curing will probably take somewhere between four and a half months to a year.

Chapter 10

More Cheeses

This chapter includes cheeses less easily classified and discussed elsewhere. Some of these are quite unusual but they're all well-known and well liked, at least in certain areas of the world. Also included are some things that aren't cheeses at all, but they are delightful, nevertheless.

Edam

Edam was first made in the vicinity of Edam, in Northern Holland. It is generally a semi-soft cheese, but it can range to hard. The flavor is pleasant, mild and sometimes slightly salty.

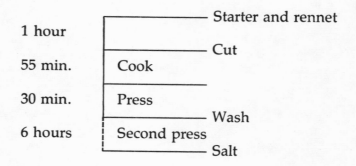

		Starter and rennet
1 hour		
		Cut
55 min.	Cook	
30 min.	Press	
		Wash
6 hours	Second press	
		Salt

You will need:

      milk (pasteurized)
      coloring (optional)
      starter
      rennet

At the start, there is a choice of whether to make modern Edam or old-fashioned Edam. Today, in most instances, the milk is partially skimmed to about 2.8 percent fat, but it used to be made from whole milk. In either case it's best to pasteurize the milk. Simply bring it to 165° F for half a minute and then let it cool. When it reaches 86° F, stabilize the temperature. Add three tablespoons of active buttermilk per gallon of milk used and coloring if desired. There is no ripening period required. All that is needed at this point is to introduce the proper organisms into the milk. Add the rennet and then stir it for two or three minutes until satisfied that it is mixed in well.

Let the curd stand undisturbed and covered for an hour. Keep the temperature as close to 86° F as possible. At the end of an hour cut the curd into ⅝-inch squares. Make sure that the knife goes all the way to the bottom, especially on the diagonal cuts, and that the same angle is maintained on the diagonal cuts. Now begin to increase the temperature slowly. During the cooking be sure to agitate every so often to keep the curds from sticking together. Increase the heat at the rate of about one and one-half minutes per degree. At the end of 15 minutes the curds and whey should have reached 95° F. Maintain the temperature of 95° F for 40 minutes, then ladle the cheese curds into the molds with a sieve or colander. Make sure to get all the curds.

Put the cheese molds in the press and apply a minimum of weight for a half-hour. Meanwhile begin heating the whey remaining in the double boiler. Increase the temperature so that in one-half hour it will reach 125° F. Then take the cheese out of the press and dip it in the warm whey. Bandage it in a cheesecloth and return it to the press. Increase the pressure on the cheese and leave it there for six hours.

Remove the cheese from the cheese press and put it in a brine solution at 50° F and sprinkle salt on its upper surface. Repeat daily and turn the cheese for a week or ten days. At the end of that period the cheese may be removed. Wipe it off and let it dry at room temperature for a couple of hours.

To cure it, store it at about 60° F for four weeks. Rub the surface with a cloth dampened in dilute salt water every other day. Keep the humidity high, about 90 percent. At the end of that four weeks it should be ready. Before that, it may be sampled by cutting out a plug and nicking ⅛-inch of cheese off the end to taste and check the flavor. It should be ready at the end of the four-week curing period. Store at a low temperature if not immediately consumed.

Queso Blanco

In Spanish this means "white cheese" and the term is used for any number of cheeses that have no coloring added to them. This particular cheese has been quite popular in some Latin American areas I have visited and you might like it for a change of pace. It uses no starter, no coloring, and no rennet. Instead of conventional methods of coagulating the curd, it is formed by adding an organic acid to hot milk. The resulting cheese is quite acidic, but when salted it loses some of that characteristic. The taste is different from that normally expected of cheese, but it is quite popular among those that are used to it.

You will need:
        milk
        lemon or lime juice
            (or some such acid)

As explained in the final chapter, cheese can be set by acid alone. Heat aids the coagulation, however, and the higher the heat the less acid required to set the curd, and the more acid added the less heat required. Making this cheese is simplicity, itself, because of this. Heat a container of milk to between 180° and 190° F. Now slowly and in small amounts add some lemon or lime juice. Without knowing the initial acidity of the milk, the precise temperature of the milk, and the strength of the acid, it is impossible to say just how much acidic acid should be added to each gallon of milk. Just add the lemon or lime juice in small quantities and mix it in well until the milk curdles.

To drain pour the curdled milk and whey into a cloth stretched across the top of a container or sink. The curds will be much too fine to be caught in a regular cheesecloth. Instead, a fairly fine-mesh linen cloth like the type used to drain Cream Cheese will have to be used. After an initial draining period the flow of whey will diminish. When this happens, scrape the sides of the cloth down with a butter knife or some similar instrument to facilitate the continued drainage of whey. To get some of the final whey out of the cheese hold the ends of the draining cloth together and twist the cloth around so it makes a bag. Continue twisting the bag so that the curd is placed under pressure. Continue applying pressure until the curd has been dried to the proper consistency for your taste.

The curd will be quite acidy and quite unlike most cheeses. This acidity can be diminished if desired by rinsing the fine curd in cold water. The taste will become more bland but the cheese will also be much more susceptible to spoilage with the acidity removed so little, if anything, is gained. The salting will remove much of that taste, anyway, and also serve to focus the flavor. Just add fine salt to the curd and mix it in. Be sure the salt is added only in small quantities to avoid a too-salty cheese. When it suits your taste it is ready.

Ever wonder what it would be like to drop in to lunch with a family several thousand years ago? What would those ancient foods taste like? This cheese gives at least part of the answer. The oldest cheese is the Arabian Kishk made from coagulated goat's milk and then dried. Andaluz is also made from goat's milk and is practically the same cheese. This is probably the cheese that David carried with him when he heard about Goliath. The cheese to be described is still being made in Andalusia. It is easy to make, ripens quickly and has a good flavor.

You will need:
> fresh goat's milk
> rennet

The milk is often stabilized at 86° to 88° F, but if you prefer you can just add the rennet mixture to the milk while it is still warm. Out of curiosity, I measured the temperature of the milk from my own goats right after milking them and found the thermometer to register 91° F. Mix the rennet with an amount of lukewarm water 30 to 40 times its own volume. Mix well and let it sit for 20 to 30 minutes undisturbed in a warm place. The container of milk could be put in a pan of warm water having a temperature as high or higher than the milk. Do not disturb until it has formed a firm curd. Notice that no starter has been added. This cheese depends on the lactic bacteria normally found in milk for its ripening and flavor characteristics.

When the curd has set sufficiently, cut it into ¼-inch to ⅜-inch cubes as explained in the second chapter. Make sure that the curd is cut through all the way to the bottom. The cuts are small and close together so the knife should be sharp to make clean cuts that won't tear the curd or run over into the next cut. After the curd is cut into small cubes, stir it gently for about ten minutes to give the cubes a chance to expel whey. Pour the curds and whey into a cheesecloth spread across the top of a container to catch the whey or alternatively into a colander. As soon as the curds stop draining, stir them a little to open up any pockets of whey that have been trapped.

When the whey has been drained pour the curds into a cheese form. These cheeses are usually fairly wide and thin, making it easier for the cheese to continue to expel whey. A cheese form six inches wide with the cheese two inches thick is probably a good average. Spread the cheese curds out in the cheese form evenly and then put the follower on top of the curds. Put the curd-filled form in the cheese press and add weight. Allow it to remain under pressure for an hour and then take the cheese out of the form. Rub the exterior with table salt or sea salt if preferred. Rub it in thoroughly and then flip the cheese over and put it back in the mold. It will be upside down now in contrast to its original position. Again press for an hour and repeat the salting process. Take the cheese out of the mold if it is firm enough to be handled. If it is still fragile, salt again and put back in the mold for another hour. Many prefer to leave the cheese in the mold overnight, but it is a matter of personal preference. Remove the cheese from the mold and put in a cool, fairly dry place to ripen. Test by tasting occasionally until it suits you. It generally starts to develop a distinctive flavor after about three days. It will usually keep in the neighborhood of two weeks.

Hand

Hand cheese is still popular with some of the kitchen cheesemakers in Germany and surrounding countries including part of Russia. It is a strong cheese with a pronounced aroma and taste. Chances are, you won't like it the very first time you try it, especially if your taste runs toward the mild cheeses. If, on the other hand, your tastes run to Limburger and similar cheeses, you might give this one a try.

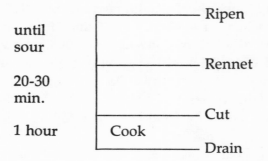

A gallon or two of whole, raw milk is needed. Add three or four tablespoons of buttermilk to the milk and allow it to remain at room temperature until it starts to taste sour but not until it develops enough acidity to form a curd by itself. Warm the milk to 86°. Dissolve some rennet in 30 to 40 times its volume of cool water and add to the milk. Enough rennet is added to cause the milk to set up in 20 to 30 minutes. This will be slightly less than would normally be required because of the greater than normal acidity. Make sure that the rennet is thoroughly mixed into the milk.

Cut the curd in large squares and then swish the knife blade back and forth through the curds and whey so that the chunks of curd are cut into small pieces. Cut them so that they are about the size of a grain of wheat. After the curd has been cut up, allow it to set in the whey for about five minutes with just enough slight agitation to keep it from matting together. During this time the curds will begin to firm just slightly and with the high acid they will start to shrink, expelling whey. At the end of five minutes begin to slowly increase the heat. Increase it at a rate of two degrees every five minutes until the temperature reaches 100° F, continuing the agitation. Hold at that point for a half an hour.

Next pour the curds and whey into a colander or a cheesecloth stretched above a container to catch the whey. The curds will have firmed considerably by the time this point is reached so they will no longer mat together as readily. Stir the curds and move them around on the cheesecloth or in the colander to open any pockets of whey that might have formed and to facilitate the rapid drainage of whey. When most of the whey has drained off spread the curds out on an absorbent cloth, a food-drying screen or something like that which will allow the curds to continue to drain individually. After the curd has drained thoroughly, it is heaped together in a container and salt is added to taste. Caraway seed is a popular addition also. The cheese is then molded in small, flat wafers by hand (hence, its name) and then put in a moist curing area with a temperature under 50° F. Part of the flavor and probably all of the odor comes from the surface ripening that takes place at this time. The surface of the cheese should be kept free from molds. After surface ripening has started, wrap them in wax paper and pack the cheese together in a box until ripening is completed.

Yogurt Cheese

This is a delightful cheese from the Mediterranean. It can be made a number of ways including one way with and one way without rennet. This description will be for making a small, individual-size portion and it will not use rennet.

Add a teaspoon of yogurt culture to two pints of milk. Slowly heat the milk and starter to between 105° and 110° F. Allow it to incubate at that temperature until the curd coagulates from the acid produced by the starter. Stir a teaspoon of salt into the curd and pour the salted yogurt into a cloth. It can be a couple of layers of cheesecloth or a loose-threaded linen cloth. Allow it to drain over a sink or pan until the whey has been expelled.

After the draining period the cheese can be put in forms and molded into squares if desired. It can be seasoned with herbs and spices depending on your taste and imagination. Want something different and low-calorie? Use this cheese in place of Cream Cheese in recipes. You might be surprised!

Egg

From Finland comes this interesting cheese. It is the equivalent of a concentrated eggnog, but without the spices.

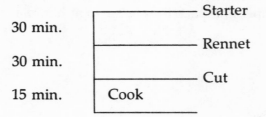

30 min.	Starter
	Rennet
30 min.	
	Cut
15 min.	Cook

You will need:
> whole milk
> buttermilk starter
> eggs (one for every quart of
>   milk used)
> rennet

Begin by choosing whole milk of a good quality. As with milk for all cheeses it should be kept as nearly free as possible of bacterial contaminants caused by unsanitary procedures. Warm the milk to 86° F and stabilize the temperature at that point.

Crack the eggs, one for every quart of milk used, in a bowl. Add five tablespoons of buttermilk starter for every gallon of milk to be used. Add the starter directly to the eggs and whip them up together until it makes a homogenous mixture. After the starter has been thoroughly mixed with the egg add it to the milk and mix it in.

Allow the mixture to ripen for half an hour at 86° F. At the end of that time add the rennet. Be sure it is mixed with an adequate amount of water and is mixed in well, then allow it to remain for another half-hour. At the end of that time the curd should be firm enough to retain its shape when pulled away from the sides of the container or to break cleanly over a finger inserted at an angle beneath the curd and lifted up.

Following the directions in the second chapter, cut the curd into cubes ⅜-inch in diameter. With gentle agitation to keep the curd from matting together, allow the curd to remain in the whey for 10 to 15 minutes to begin the expulsion of whey and firm the curd slightly. Now begin to slowly increase the heat at the rate of one degree every five minutes until the temperature has been increased to 92° F. This should be in half an hour.

Pour the curds and whey into a colander or a cheesecloth stretched across the top of a container. Allow to drain for five to ten minutes. Spread the curd out in the colander or cheesecloth and shift the curd once or twice to open any pockets of whey that might have formed. Add to the curd three teaspoons of salt per gallon of milk used, a third at a time, and mix it in well. Put the curd in a cheese form one to two inches deep. Put the follower on and add weight. Allow the cheese to remain under pressure for an hour, then take it out and reverse it. Put it under pressure in the new position for an hour and then take it out of the press. Store in a cool place (about 55° F) with a humidity of about 85 percent until it ripens to your taste.

Feta

Feta is cheese of the mountains of Greece. Its chief distinguishing characteristic is that it is pickled. Its manufacture is quite close to Queso de Cabra, which is probably the most ancient true cheese. It is very likely that this is just a variation of that same cheese passed down from generation to generation from ancient times and then preserved by the shepherds in the mountains of Greece. To this day it remains, in certain areas, the main soft cheese of these people. It is soft and ready to eat in less than a week.

You will need:
>   rennet
>   fresh milk

As might be expected for a cheese made in relatively primitive circumstances, it is easy and fast to make. Although in Greece the cheese is made from a ewe's milk, it can also be made from goat or cow milk. Heat the milk and stabilize the temperature at 90° to 95° F. No starter is added to this cheese, but add enough rennet to coagulate the milk in 20 to 30 minutes. Allow the renneted milk to set until it will break cleanly over a finger inserted at an angle under the curd and then lifted up.

Cut the curd into cubes about ½-inch in diameter. Then pour the curds and what whey has formed in that period of time into a cloth bag made of muslin or maybe of something having a little more open weave such as clean burlap. Pick up the four corners of the cloth and twist so that it forms a bag with the curd held in the middle. Continue to twist this bag so that the curd is put under pressure. This will help in the removal of

whey. After the initial whey has been removed, suspend the cloth by the corners and let it hang up for four or five hours. At the end of that time the curd will have matted together under the initial compression of the curd and the continued draining under its own weight.

Remove it from the bag and slice it into inch slices. Cover each slice with a good layer of salt on both sides and let it set overnight. After that time the curd is resalted but with slightly less salt this time and packed in a container such as a crock. The highly-salted cheese is left there for a period of about five days and it is then ready to use.

Kefir Cheese

Kefir cheese can be made in several ways and here is the easiest. It is quite bland so it is ideal to mix with other, more positive cheeses. This, too, is a cheese that can be made without benefit of rennet.

You will need:
    kefir
    cheesecloth

Strain the Kefir grains out of the cultured Kefir milk and put into a heating container. (See also Kefir, next chapter.) It can be heated directly on the stove, but it must be watched carefully so that it won't boil over or burn the milk sugar. Slowly and carefully heat the Kefir until it is almost to the boiling point. When foam begins to appear on the surface retard the heating but allow it to continue until the whole surface is covered. Let the mixture stand for 30 seconds and then put the cooking container in some cool water for just a few seconds to cool slightly. Put in a spot where it can remain undisturbed for 12 hours. Make sure that the container is covered so that it will not be contaminated.

Stretch a couple of layers of cheesecloth across the top of a pan and pour the coagulated Kefir on top. Allow it to drain and add salt and whatever other flavorings you feel are appropriate.

Potato Cheese

This is an interesting little cheese made originally in Central Germany. Not only is it good, it is also a perfect way to use up leftover mashed potatoes. This is one of those cheeses that has never really been standardized and it is, in fact, little-known. It is not a good keeper and should be used within a couple of weeks.

until sour		Starter
20-30 min.		Rennet
10 min.	Soak	Cut
30 min.		Drain
+/− 1 hour		Second cut
		Add potatoes

You will need:
 milk
 potatoes
 rennet
 buttermilk starter
 salt
 caraway seeds (optional)

For each gallon of milk to be used add five tablespoons of buttermilk starter. The milk needn't be pasteurized but it should be free from off-flavors. Allow it to set in a warm place for several hours or until the milk starts to have a definite sour flavor. Bring the temperature of the milk up to 86° F and then add the rennet. Make sure it is diluted with an adequate amount of water and mix in the milk thoroughly. Let it set 20 to 30 minutes or until the curd is strong enough to break cleanly over your finger. Cut the curd into ¼-inch cubes and let it set for ten minutes, stirring to keep the curd from matting together.

Now pour into a cheesecloth suspended over a pan or into a colander. Allow the curd to drain for 20 minutes. By this time the curd will have matted together. Take the curd out and, using a kitchen knife, dice it into ¼-inch cubes. They needn't be perfect. Spread the diced curd out on a clean cloth to dry. Don't pile the curd on top of itself; instead spread it around.

The potatoes should be boiled and peeled. Also mash them if not already in that form. After the curd has been allowed to drain on the clean cloth for 20 minutes at room temperature, mix the curd and mashed potatoes together in equal portions. Later this mixture can be varied to suit your tastes. Add salt to taste and mix it all up thoroughly. Let it ripen at room temperature for two days, mix it up again, place it in a cheese mold and add weight. Leave it in the mold for a day, then take it out and let it cure for one to two weeks.

Fromage Fort

Fromage Fort is for cheesemakers who think they have attempted everything possible to get a different flavored cheese. The unusual characteristic of this cheese is that the curd is cooked; not just heated to 90° or 100° F in whey to firm the curd, but actually cooked!

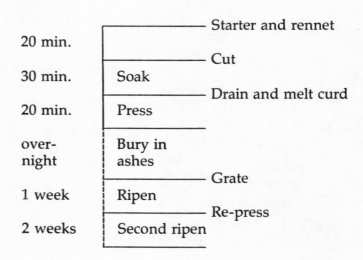

		Starter and rennet
20 min.		
		Cut
30 min.	Soak	
		Drain and melt curd
20 min.	Press	
over-night	Bury in ashes	
		Grate
1 week	Ripen	
		Re-press
2 weeks	Second ripen	

You will need:
> buttermilk starter
> rennet
> skim milk

Add a cup of well-ripened buttermilk starter to every gallon of milk used. If the buttermilk has sufficient acidity to have formed a curd, break the soft curd up and shake well to make a thick mixture. Heat the milk to 86° F and add the starter. Mix it in well and then add enough rennet to coagulate the curd in 20 to 30 minutes. Allow the curd to coagulate until it forms a soft, jellylike curd. Cut the curd into strips ¼-inch in diameter—strips that reach all the way to the bottom of the container. Do not make the diagonal cuts. After the cuts have been made, stir the curd to break the strips into smaller pieces. After stirring for 10 minutes with the temperature maintained at 86° F, increase the agitation and stir with a pastry whisk or something similar which will break the curd into small pieces. Agitate to keep the curd from matting together. Let the curd set to expel whey and shrink and firm up slightly. At the end of the half-hour period pour the curds and whey into a cheesecloth-lined colander and allow to drain. Spread the curds out on the bottom of the colander to help drainage. If the amount of curd is large and it is piled up, shift the curds occasionally to open up any whey pockets that might have been trapped inside.

When the curds are thoroughly drained, melt them in a pan over low heat. This done, pour the melted cheese onto a cloth. When the cheese has solidified, it should be pressed either by putting weight on the melted curd or by lining a small cheese mold with cloth and then pouring the curd into it. After the cheese is pressed for 20 minutes it may be taken out. Traditionally the cloth is removed and the cheese is buried in dry wood ashes to remove even more moisture. Allow the cheese to remain covered in the ashes overnight, then dust the ashes off and, keeping in mind that there will be a small amount of lye in the ashes, rinse well in cold water. Grate the cheese into medium-size pieces and store it to ripen with the temperature held to between 60° and 65° F for a week. Salt, pepper or other flavorings, depending on personal preference, are then added to the shredded curd. The spices and cheese should be thoroughly mixed up with a little buttermilk starter and then pressed with the use of a lot of pressure to firm it up. The cheese is then allowed to ripen for another two weeks or to taste. Keep it in a room where the temperature is held at about 55° to 60° F. Unlike most cheeses, the humidity should be kept low to encourage the cheese to become well dried.

Smoked Cheese

Smoking has long been a method of preserving foods. The incomplete combustion of wood releases a variety of mold and bacteria-inhibiting compounds such as acids, aldehydes and phenols. Smoking will increase the longevity of cheeses by coating them with these substances and by also drying them out to a certain extent, but the real gain is flavor. Here is how to smoke cheeses with equipment you can put together for pennies in a few minutes. The procedure is the same as for smoking meats. The items needed are two cardboard boxes, a small can such as a tuna fish can, a hot plate or candle, a wire grill and some hardwood sawdust.

The box used to hold the cheese will have to have some provision for opening it so the cheese can be turned periodically. Use an empty cardboard soup case having a top cut open on three sides so the top can function as a door. Stand the box on its end so the lid will open toward you. Push two stiff pieces of wire through the sides to support the wire grill or, if you like, put the cheese directly on the wires. Cut several small holes in the top to let smoke out and a fairly large hole in the bottom to let the smoke in.

The bottom box should have a six or eight-inch hole at the top to allow smoke into the upper box. At the opposite end (just above the bottom) it should have a couple of small holes close to the electric hot plate allowing air to enter.

A good-quality cheese should be chosen. The smoke adds flavor, but it doesn't hide defects. Put the cheese on the grill or wires and tape the door shut. Add damp hardwood sawdust to the tuna can on top of the burner and turn on the heat. Keep the heat low, just enough to keep the sawdust smoking well. Low heat is the real secret of smoking. If the cheese becomes too hot it will sweat butterfat. Smoking should not cook or even

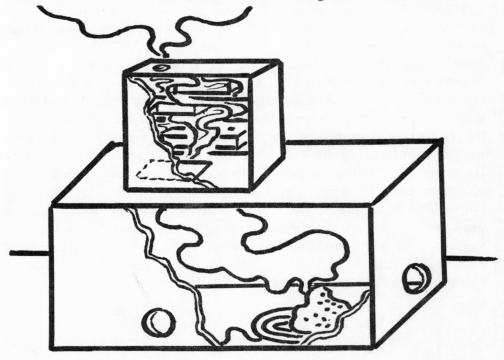

SMOKING CHEESE

really heat, only cover with smoke and dry slightly. Turn the cheeses every hour. Smoke for four to six hours and add one hour if the cheese is mild.

Can liquid smoke be used? Sure, but most people find cheese that was actually smoked the old-time way to be definitely better and more flavorful.

Soy Milk

A milk made from soybeans can be used in the same way as regular milk. There are various ways to make this milk, but since soybeans and soybean products are hard for the body to utilize unless cooked it is suggested that it be cooked at the time of manufacture to make its use in cheesemaking more convenient later on. To one cup of soy flour add three cups of water. Mix it well and then let it set for two or three hours. Then cook it 40 minutes in a double boiler and next strain it. Another method is to let a cup of soybeans soak overnight, drain off the water and run it through a food blender. Add three cups of water and cook for 15 minutes at a slow boil, then strain off the liquid.

Soy milk has a sort of beany taste when made at home but in the commercial product this taste has been removed. It is possible to develop a taste for soy milk but in the meantime its users can flavor it with malt, chocolate, etc. The main use of soy milk in the western world is as a milk substitute for those allergic to dairy products. It should be noted that soy milk is not as complete as regular milk.

Tofu

Tofu is a cheese made from soy milk rather than cow's milk. It can be allowed to sour naturally or the juice of a lemon for every two cups of soy milk can be used. If it is made from uncooked soy milk, the cheese should be cooked before it is eaten. After the soy milk has coagulated, the whey will have to be drained off through a cheesecloth just as with regular cheese. If the cheese is not used within a couple of days it should be stored in brine in a cool place until it is used.

Other products can be made from soy milk. Soy yogurt can be made just as in making regular yogurt. Use a teaspoon of regular yogurt for a starter and then incubate as for regular yogurt.

Butter

Butter is made by using almost any form of agitation, from using a butter churn to shaking the cream in a bottle. If you prefer butter from ripened cream, stir a spoonful of active buttermilk into the cream and mix it in well. Allow it to ripen and then proceed with the general instructions. Ripening also makes it churn more easily.

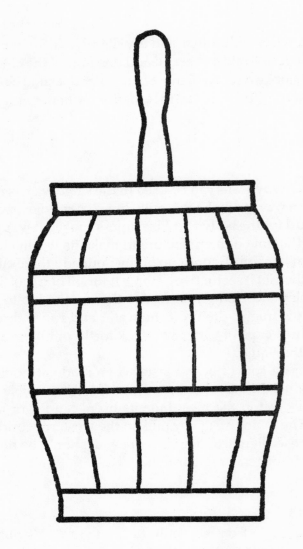

The cream should be cool, but not cold. Put cream in a churn, bottle, or even use an egg beater if you like. Agitate until the small globules of butterfat stick together and become lumpy. Slow the agitation at this point. Put the coagulated butterfat in a bowl and mash and work it around to push out the small pockets of buttermilk that have inevitably been trapped inside. As the milk forms, pour it off to avoid its working back in. When most of the buttermilk has been removed pour cold water into the bowl and continue to work the butter around. This will get the rest of the milk out of the butter. Failure to remove all the milk will cause the butter to spoil.

The butter will taste better and keep longer if salted. Add fine salt to taste and make sure it is thoroughly mixed in. If wanting a deeper color of yellow, or if, in the case of goat cream, you object to white butter, add coloring to it.

To clarify butter, heat it over low heat. Skim the foamy part that rises off the surface. It can be used in cooking or for other purposes. The part that remains is the clarified portion.

This is something you will probably never experience unless you make it yourself. It is actually a semi-solidified cream product that has a distinctly different flavor caused by partially-burned milk sugar.

Start by allowing the cream to rise in a cool place in a metal container suitable for use in heating the milk and cream. Traditionally it was a wide, rather shallow pan. When the cream has risen, put the container in another pan of water on the stove. Often this double boiler wasn't used but it allows some margin of error and it is assumed you will have a double boiler anyway for the cheeses. Now heat to about 175° to 190° F. A sort of scum will start to appear on the surface. Hold this temperature for at least half an hour or you won't have anything except wrinkled cream because the flavor won't develop.

After a half-hour or slightly longer, take it off the heat. Immediately cool by placing it in cold, running water, or better still, a pan of ice water. Now all that remains is to skim the clotted cream off the top with a spoon and use it with sugar or strawberries, peaches, etc. Once you have tried this, its taste will suggest new uses.

This is one of the easiest cheeses to make and it is quite good. You can use Devonshire Clotted Cream and then just make cheese by following the directions for cream cheese. Another method is to let the Devonshire cream set in a cool place until the cream firms up. It is then ladled into open-ended molds and allowed to drain on straw or other perforated mats. When firm the cheese is ready and can be consumed immediately.

Like unusual cheeses? If so, these may be for you. Actually they aren't cheeses in the usual sense of the word. There are those who would make a case that they are more closely related to maple syrup. In a sense they are, because they are made by condensing the milk sugar and other whey constituents into solid form. Gjetost is cheese made from part goat milk whey and cow milk whey. Ekte Gjetost (genuine goat cheese) means that it is made from 100 percent goat milk whey. Gjetost—the national cheese of Norway—is said to comprise approximately half the cheese consumed there. The very similar Mytost is popular throughout the Scandinavian countries and is made from whey taken from cow milk. When a small amount of whole milk, or even better, about 10 percent cream is added to the whey, a smoother, creamier product results which is called Primost (Quality Cheese) or Fløtost.

What will you have if you do make one of these cheeses? A mildly sweet to sweet-sour cheese that consists of milk sugar, protein, fat, and whatever minerals that have not been utilized in the curds when they were removed.

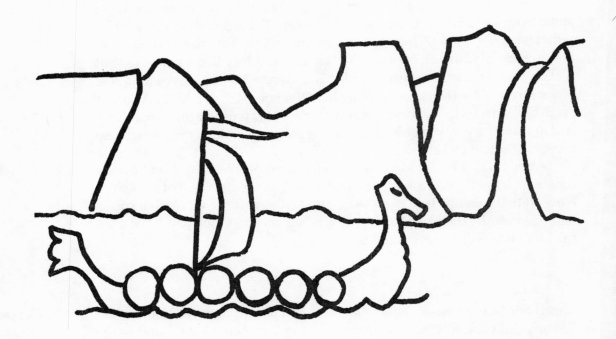

Gjetost

You will need to use the whey from cheddar or some other cheese, and it should be as fresh as possible. The sweeter the whey—that is, the less it has been allowed to ripen—the more likely the final product will lack sourness. The sourness, if it does develop, can to a certain extent be overcome by adding a little baking soda.

All that is required is to reduce the volume of whey by boiling. This should be done carefully and with stirring, especially in the latter stages to avoid burning the delicate milk sugars. This is more easily accomplished at higher altitudes. The volume should be reduced to one-fourth that of the original. During the cooking, albumin will rise to the surface in the form of a scum. Skim this off and when the volume has been reduced to about one-third that of the original and it has a thick, smooth consistency, stir the albumin back in.

After the volume is reduced to about one-quarter that of the original, or when the temperature has reached about 240 degrees, pour it into a bowl and stir to prevent the formation of sugar crystals. Pour on waxed paper or a greased plate and allow it to cool like candy. The sugar should have caramelized and it will have a brownish color.

Two important variations might be worth trying. Adding from 3 to 10 percent cream or even a little milk before the cooking begins gives a mellower final product. Some also add as much as 10 percent brown sugar to increase the final sweetness.

Ricotta

Ricotta is probably the most popular of the whey cheeses. Two types of Ricotta can be made by following the same directions, depending on whether skim or whole milk is used. Skim milk makes the dry type and whole milk produces the fresh variety.

To start with, you will need some relatively sweet cheese whey—it should not be excessively acid. It should be made into Ricotta as soon as possible after it is drawn from the curd. You will also need some sour whey that has been allowed to develop more acidity or, alternatively, you can use some other acid coagulant, such as lemon or lime juice. Using the juice from these fruits will give a different taste though. Also needed will be either whole or skim milk.

Begin by heating the sweet whey. Add ¼ cup of either whole or skim milk for each quart of whey used. The choice of whether to use whole or skim milk will depend on whether a dry or fresh Ricotta is to be made. Heat the whey and milk to about 200° F. In absence of a thermometer registering that high, estimate the temperature by watching for bubbles starting to form. When these bubbles rise, the whey is close to the temperature required. When the whey reaches this temperature, stir in some of the sour whey or similar acid coagulant, such as lemon or lime juice. A scum of coagulated albumin will appear on the top of the whey. This should be skimmed off with a slotted spoon or piece of cheesecloth. Continue to add small amounts of the coagulating agent until the ricotta ceases to appear on the top of the whey.

Put the coagulated whey in a cheesecloth and hang it over a sink or similar area and allow it to drain. After the ricotta has drained and cooled, transfer it to a bowl and add salt to taste. Next add some buttermilk starter to the curd and mix it in well—don't add so much though that it will make the cheese overly moist, just enough so that a lactic starter will be introduced to the curd to aid in the ripening characteristics.

Line a cheese mold with cheesecloth and fill the mold with curd. Put the follower on top and put it in the cheese press under weight. Allow it to remain in the press for six or seven hours under fairly heavy pressure. If desired, the cheese can then be eaten immediately. If skim milk has been used for a dry Ricotta, the cheese must be dried. This is done by letting it stand in a very warm area (90° to 100° F.) where there is little humidity. An alternate method is to put the cheese in a food dryer. When dried this cheese is often used for grating. These cheeses usually weigh about five pounds, but since so little cheese is obtained from the whey they can be made in any size that is convenient.

Chapter 11

Cultured Milk Products

Is there really any practical use for fermented milk products? Milk is a natural for home storage because of its high protein content. Not only is the level high but its quality is of the best. Unfortunately, for all its attributes, there are some who cannot utilize it because they lack an enzyme, lactase, that the body uses to break the milk down. In America and West Europe those with this impairment represent only about two to eight percent of the population, but in other parts of the world the percentage runs as high as 60 to 80. In America some of the minority groups have a high intolerance for sweet milk. As a person gets older his ability to produce lactase generally declines, and sometimes this may develop an intolerance for milk. The person who feels uncomfortable after drinking milk or has stomach cramps or diarrhea may suffer from this intolerance. The only way to tell for sure is to take a lactose intolerance test from a doctor.

Fermented milk products, such as yogurt, buttermilk, cheeses and Kefir are very low in lactose so these may be used as substitutes for regular milk without ill effects in cases of lactose intolerance. An advantage to these products is that they provide variety. Of course, as the taste changes, the nutritional value also changes.

Lactose intolerance isn't the only reason that fermented milk products are useful. The acid conditions prevalent in these products also prevent or inhibit the multiplication of some pathogenic organisms, especially those that cause dysentery. *S. typhi* and *shigella* are killed when placed in yogurt, which explains why some treatments of stomach disorders caused by bacterial action call for the regular consumption of some type of fermented milk product.

Still another reason for the use of fermented milk products is that they keep without refrigeration for a long period of time. In some parts of the world where people seem to attain long life, yogurt is often one of their main foods. While there is little reason to credit their longevity to yogurt, there is no reason to ignore the advantages of the fermented milk products either.

Buttermilk

When speaking of buttermilk it is well to be aware that it can refer to several different products. Regular buttermilk is simply the liquid portion left from the cream when the butterfat is converted into butter. Bulgarian buttermilk is a milk containing a culture solely of *Lactobacillus bulgaricus*. Throughout this book, though, and almost without exception, the term "buttermilk" refers to the American cultured variety. This consists of a lactic acid-producing organism, or perhaps a combination of lactic acid-producing organisms plus other organisms that add to and modify flavor and aroma.

Making buttermilk is very easy. All that is needed is a container of active, commercial cultured buttermilk added to a small quantity of milk. The milk is then placed in a warm place where it would naturally sour. As the organisms in the commercial buttermilk increase, they produce acid preventing other organisms from growing, although when a high acid point is reached, they finally inhibit their own growth. Because of this ability to preclude other bacterial activity, buttermilk is useful in temporarily preserving milk in warm weather when other means are not available.

After sufficient acid has developed, the milk will form a curd, as explained elsewhere in this book. But unless there is a specific reason for allowing the acidity to increase to that point, the buttermilk should be refrigerated well before then. If allowed to continue, the curd will gradually turn acrid. Even though this is a fermented milk product no alcohol develops.

The ripening can take place in any clean container that is unaffected by acid. Buttermilk is usually cultured at around 70° F. Higher temperatures can be used but some of the secondary aroma-producing bacteria will eventually die out. To maintain this temperature it is often enough to place the container of buttermilk in a warm place overnight. A vacuum bottle or the alfalfa box described at the end of the chapter also works exceptionally well for incubating the cultured milks found in this chapter.

If a buttermilk has developed an off-flavor it generally means that either the milk had some off-flavors to begin with or, more likely, there is some source of contamination. If any organisms other than the ones especially cultured appear, their presence will usually be shown by off-flavors or odors. If this is the case the buttermilk should be discarded and a new culture procured from a reliable source such as a bottle of fresh buttermilk from a reputable dairy.

Yogurt

Yogurt is traditionally made from a number of milks including sheep, goat, mare and cow. Like most fermented milks it is easy to make, given a good culture of the proper type. Often the milk is pasteurized to destroy any bacteria that might compete with the lactobacilli in the milk and that might impair the taste or, in some extreme cases, even add toxins. Traditionally, the milk was heated until bubbles began to form around the edges of the container. It was then cooled down and when an elbow put in the milk felt neither hot nor cold, it was ready to be inoculated. Often it was tested for temperature by sprinkling on a wrist as one would a bottle of baby's milk. The real secret, besides using a good-quality starter, is to keep the milk at the proper temperature. Even though it is a heat-loving culture it should be kept under 115° F so that it won't kill the culture.

The starter can be bought in dry, granular form from many health food stores or else you can buy a container of good-quality commercial yogurt and use a teaspoon of it as a starter. Although at this time most cultures don't list the particular bacteria involved, this may change in the future. When it can be found, a very good starter is one that combines *L. bulgaricus, L. acidophilus* and *Streptoccus thermophilus.* Use the starter sparingly because too much will affect the texture by making it lumpy.

Incubation is most efficiently carried out at temperatures between 105° and 110° F. At this temperature and providing the milk is fresh, ripening will take place in from one to two hours. The longer the yogurt is incubated the more acidy and the stronger the taste will be. If the yogurt is over-incubated, not only will the taste be impaired, but it will become tough. If the temperature is allowed to cool, the bacterial action will cease and it will have to be rewarmed. It is easier to keep the temperature in the correct range than to try to rewarm. After the yogurt has started to incubate move it as little as possible for best results.

Incubation is made quite simple with the modern yogurt incubators on the market. It isn't really necessary to buy one, however. A wide-mouth vacuum bottle will do an excellent job. Just heat the milk to the desired temperature, say about 110° F, add the starter and pour into the vacuum bottle. Some of the initial heat loss can be avoided by rinsing the bottle out with hot water first. In many rural areas of the world where milk cultures were regularly incubated, the cultures were often put in bottles and then covered in some way to minimize heat loss. A straw box was often provided for this purpose. The containers of culture were placed in a straw box wrapped in soft wool blankets to keep the heat in. Feather bed comforters were used in some cases. If nothing else, the container can be wrapped in a wool blanket or several layers of newspaper and then some old blankets. Another method is to put the container into a pan of water, the container resting on a jar lid, and put it on low heat—or incubate it in the top of a double boiler over very low heat. But remember, if the temperature gets over 115° F the culture is killed and you have to start over again.

Save enough of the yogurt for a starter to put in the next batch. Eventually, though, one bacteria will become dominant and you will need a new commercial starter. For best results, first wash all the containers to be used thoroughly to minimize the danger of introduction of unwanted bacteria. Use containers of inert material such as glass or stainless steel, and store the finished product in a cool place, preferably between 35° and 40° F, until used. Try to use it up within a week to keep it from becoming too acidy.

Yogurt is very popular and good when fruit is added to it when it loses a little of its low-calorie benefits. Commercially, the fruit flavor is usually concentrated at the bottom to avoid a lumpy texture. In the kitchen this is avoided by mixing the fruit in a blender and then adding it just before the yogurt is eaten.

Kefir

Mentioned by Marco Polo, Kefir is still less well-known than many other forms of fermented milk, possibly because the Moslems who believed that it would lose its strength if it was used by infidels, kept it from the outside world. It has a very low curd tension and so is more easily digested. Like yogurt it helps reestablish normal flora in the intestinal tract after they have been lost, usually from prolonged use of antibiotics.

Kefir consists of three kinds of lactic-acid bacteria plus a lactose-fermenting yeast. It ferments somewhat more slowly than yogurt, which is often an advantage. Unlike yogurt, however, a start is not made from some of the fermented milk; instead, small grains which form in the bottom of the mixture called ''grains of the Prophet Mohammed'' by the Moslems, are used. Also, unlike yogurt, you do not have to renew the starter from time to time.

Put one-half to one cup of the Kefir grains in a quart of milk. The more grains the thicker the finished product and the faster the action. Low fat or skim milk works best. Incubate for two or three days at 65° to 75° F. The grains will multiply so that pretty soon there will be more than needed. Put these in a sieve and rinse them briefly but thoroughly in cold running water. Surplus grains are then stored for making the next batch of Kefir; they may be stored by freezing or drying. Kefir tastes a great deal like yogurt, but is a drink rather than a soft solid, and it is smooth and creamy. Like yogurt it can be flavored with fruit.

The alfalfa box is simply a container kept in a well-insulated box. Sometimes in the past it was called a "Wyoming wife" and used in frontier areas in much the same way as a vacuum bottle. It is capable of keeping hot things hot and cold things cold quite a long time. It is also ideal for incubating starters and cultured milk products.

To make one, first procure a box about four inches wider and longer than the container to be used for incubating milk. In choosing this container be sure to pick one large enough to incubate an adequate amount of milk—a two-quart container is a popular size. It should be of stainless steel, glass or some other acid-resistant material. A quantity of green alfalfa and some ½-inch chicken wire are also needed.

The box can be made of cardboard, but wooden ones are preferable, being more durable. An orange crate or fruit box will do if the wooden slats are close enough together to retain the hay. The box will also need a lid and for that reason many cheesemakers make their own boxes. Make the wooden box about 18 inches by 18 inches by 24 inches deep. All four sides are covered with boards or plywood and then the top is cut off for the lid.

Once the box and lid are ready, the next thing is to fill it rather loosely with *green* alfalfa along the sides, but packed tighter on the bottom. Put the pot into the box and hollow out a hole to fit it snugly. Now pack in green alfalfa all around the container. A little more may have to be added to the bottom so that the top of the pot is at least level with the top of the box, if not a little higher. If the container has a protruding handle, enough space must be provided so it does not interfere with the lid when it is put on. There's usually no problem with a bail-type handle.

Stuff the box lid loosely full of alfalfa and, with the container in the box, push it snugly closed. Continue to take it off and rearrange the hay until it fits the top of the pot snugly. To hold the alfalfa against the lid, the last step is to tack chicken wire across the bottom of the box lid. For a good fit, avoid stretching it too tightly. It may be necessary to snip a wire here and there to insure a good fit. When fit properly, the lid of the box will be flush with the box's upper edges and there will be no cracks between the two to defeat its insulation properties. If the alfalfa pushes up slightly from the bottom and/or down from the top, as is often the case, it might be necessary to add some weight to the top of the box. If necessary, use some fastening system, such as trunk locks or even a belt fastened over the top, to keep it in place. Let the alfalfa dry, preferably with the pot in place, so that it will dry to the desired dimensions.

In use, put the milk and a starter in the incubating container and heat them to the desired temperature. Then put the container inside the alfalfa box and put on the lid. If put together properly, the box should keep the incubating milk warm for hours.

Chapter 12

Recipes

Included here are some classic recipes as well as some of the newer ones. All in all, it is hoped they will offer new and interesting ways to use a very old and delicious food. They depend mainly on the so-called basic cheeses.

SWISS FONDUE

In a fondue pot, put:

    2 c. dry white wine

Bring wine to a simmer; do not boil. Meanwhile, toss together:

    1 lb. naturally aged Swiss cheese, coarsely grated

    3 tbl. flour

Add to the gently simmering wine about 3 tablespoons at a time, stirring well between each addition with a wooden spoon till cheese melts. Bring the fondue to a simmer briefly. Add:

    3 tbl. kirsch

Stir in. Serve with chunks of firm French bread dipped in. As the fondue progresses, it might become thick. If so, add a little *hot* white wine. Makes about 3 cups.

CHEESE PUFFS

In a heavy-bottomed saucepan, bring to boil:

   1 c. water
   6 tbl. butter, sliced (for easy melting)
   1 tsp. salt
   Pinch of pepper

When water is still bubbling, and butter is melted, beat in directly with wooden spoon:

   1 c. flour

To evaporate extra moisture, place pan back over heat, and stir until mixture leaves sides and bottom of pan and spoon. Remove from heat, make a well in center of dough and beat in thoroughly, one at a time:

   4 eggs

While still warm, stir in:

   ¾ c. Swiss cheese, finely grated
   ¼ c. Parmesan or Romano cheese, grated

Spoon out dough onto lightly greased baking sheet about 1 teaspoon in a puff, at least 2 inches apart. Glaze the tops only with:

   1 egg yolk mixed with 2 tbl. water

Sprinkle puff tops with:

   about ½ c. Swiss cheese, grated, about ½ tsp. per puff

Bake at 425°, about 20 minutes, pierce each puff to let out steam, return to turned-off oven for 10 minutes.

QUICHE LORRAINE

For pastry shell, blend in bowl:

    1¼ c. flour

    1 tsp. salt

Cut in:

    ½ c. shortening

Stir in:

    Just enough cold water to hold together

Roll out and place in 8 or 9-in. pie tin or plate.

For custard, blend in bowl:

    1 c. cream

    4 egg yolks

Fry till crisp:

    1 lb. bacon

Sauté till soft, but not brown:

    1 lg. onion, sliced thinly

Arrange bacon and onion in pie shell with:

    ½ lb. Swiss cheese, grated coarsely

Top with custard, bake at 375°, 35 to 45 minutes.

FONDUTA ALLA PIEMONTESE

Place in bowl, let stand overnight:

    1 lb. mozzarella cheese, diced small

    Enough milk to cover

Place in double boiler over hot, not boiling, water. Beat vigorously till cheese is dissolved. Stir in, stirring constantly:

    5 egg yolks

    ¼ tsp. salt

    Pinch of white pepper

Cook for another minute or two, stirring constantly. The classic Italian garnish is sliced white truffles. Fonduta should be creamy-thick.

CHEESE CROUTONS

Mix together:

    ⅔ c. soft butter

    ½ c. Parmesan, grated

Spread on top of:

    12 slices stale French bread

Cut bread into cubes, and drop cubes in a hot, not smoky, skillet. Shake pan vigorously to prevent sticking, and turn croutons as they need it, adding a tablespoon of butter to the pan. Remove and serve on soup or salads.

Stir in a heavy-bottomed saucepan over high heat:

     2 c. mashed potatoes

Stir until potatoes begin to cloud the bottom, to remove moisture. Beat in:

     3 eggs

     ¼ c. Parmesan, grated

     ½ c. Swiss cheese

     1 tsp. salt

     ¼ tsp. white pepper

     Pinch of nutmeg

Stir in to form a thick dough:

     ½ to 1 c. flour

Form into very small (½ to 1 tsp. size) balls, drop, one at a time, into:

     1 gallon hot boiling water

When the dumplings come to the top, they are done. Drain on paper towels. Place the done dumplings onto an oven-proof platter with about:

     ⅓ c. soft butter in the bottom

Toss the dumplings gently in the butter, sprinkle a little more Parmesan on the top, bake at 400° about 8 minutes.

**CHEESE
GNOCCHI**

VEAL PARMESAN

Simmer 10 minutes:

> 1 small can tomato sauce
> ¼ tsp. basil
> ¼ tsp. thyme
> 1 tsp. sugar
> Dash of salt
> 1 tbl. white wine
> 1 clove garlic, whole
> 1 tsp. butter

Remove garlic bud and keep hot. Meanwhile dip:

> 4 5-oz. veal cutlets, ¼" thick

Into:

> 1 egg
> 2 tbl. water

Drain on a rack to remove excess batter and then dip into:

> ⅔ c. fine bread crumbs

Sauté cutlets in a little shortening till golden-brown on both sides, drain on paper. Then in a baking pan, set the cutlets without overlapping, pour the tomato sauce over the veal, and sprinkle with:

> 3 tbl. Parmesan, grated

Bake at 325°, about 1 hr. and 10 minutes, until the cutlets are tender. Now place on each cutlet:

> 4 ⅛" slices mozzarella cheese

Replace in the oven just long enough for the cheese to melt. Serves 4.

WELSH RABBIT

In saucepan over *low* heat, stir constantly till melted:

> 2 c. sharp cheddar, grated
> ½ c. beer, flat, with no foam

Stir till smooth and add:

> 1 tsp. dry mustard
> 1 tbl. Worcestershire sauce

Add a small amount of hot cheese to:

> 1 beaten egg

Stir till blended, add to cheese mixture, and stir over *low* heat till thick and smooth. Serve over toast, makes about 3 cups.

CREOLE CREAM CHEESE

Mix together:

> 1 lb. cottage cheese, large-curded
> 1 c. heavy, thick cream
> 1 tbl. sugar

Serve with a mixture of soft, fresh fruit, pitted and cut into pieces, and very good for brunches. Makes about 3 cups.

114

Beat together:

      3 eggs, lightly beaten

      1½ c. milk

Beat in till barely mixed:

      1 c. flour

      4½ tsp. baking powder

      Dash of salt

Now pour ¼ c. of batter into an 8″ frying pan that has ½ tbl. butter melted in it, tilting to spread. Cook about 1½ minutes till pancake is brown, flip over and cook other side. Make about 1 more pancake out of the batter. Fill with:

      2 eggs, beaten

      1½ lbs. ricotta cheese

      3 tbl. butter, melted

      ½ c. sour cream

      Dash of salt

      ½ c. superfine sugar

      1 tsp. lemon rind

      1½ tbl. cinnamon

Place off-center on each blintz, roll, place in a buttered baking dish, and sprinkle blintzes with:

      ¼ c. superfine sugar

      1 tsp. cinnamon

Spread top of blintzes with:

      2 c. sour cream

Bake at 350°, for 30 minutes. Serve immediately. Serves 6.

Make the pancake batter of the Cheese Blintzes, and make the pancakes. Fill them with:

½ lb. dried apricots

3 c. cold water

Cook gently for about 45 minutes. Add:

½ c. sugar

Continue cooking until mixture thickens, about 20 minutes longer. Then add:

1 tbl. rum

2 tbl. cream

½ c. cottage or ricotta cheese

Roll up neatly. Sprinkle with cinnamon sugar and cream.

HUNGARIAN CHEESECAKE

In a bowl, place:

1¼ c. flour

Cut in:

1 cube butter

Add, and knead until smooth:

1 tbl. lemon juice

1½ tbl. sour cream

2 egg yolks

Cover and chill in refrigerator. Meanwhile, cook:

2 med.-sized potatoes in their skins

Let cool, peel. Put through the potato ricer. In the bowl containing the crust dough, put:

4 egg yolks

4 tbl. butter

1¼ c. sugar

Beat together. Add:

1 tbl. vanilla

1 lb. (1 pt.) cottage cheese

2 tbl. milk

1 tbl. cream of wheat

Stir together. Now fold in:

4 egg whites, beaten stiff

½ cup sultana raisins

1½ tsp. lemon rind, grated

10 or so blanched almonds, sliced (opt.)

Roll out dough to a thickness of ¼" thick, saving about ⅓ of the dough. Place the crust in a 8 or 9" spring-form pan. Pour cheese mixture into the crust-lined pan, and put rolled strips of dough, from the reserved third of dough, in a sort of lattice design. Bake at 350° for 30 minutes, and at 300° for another 30 minutes.

Mix together, then shape into balls about 1 tsp. large:

> ½ c. Swiss cheese, grated
> 2 tbl. Parmesan or Romano cheese, grated
> 1 egg white, lightly beaten
> Dash of Tabasco

Roll in:

> Fine bread crumbs

Drop in hot, deep oil. Remove when they puff and begin to brown. Drain on paper towels. Serve soon.

DELICIOUS CHEESEBALLS

Mix together till smooth:

> 1 c. cheddar, sharp, and finely grated
> 6 oz. cream cheese
> ½ c. sour cream

Add, mix all together:

> 1 sm. onion, very finely chopped
> 3 tbl. caraway, or chopped nuts
> 1 tbl. white wine or 2 tbl. beer
> 1 tbl. prepared mustard
> 2 tbl. paprika
> ¼ t. salt

Form into ball, and roll in additional seeds or chopped nuts. Makes about 3 cups.

CHEDDAR CHEESE BALL

Mash all together till smooth:

> 8 oz. blue cheese, roquefort, or Gorgonzola
>   (or portions of all three)
> 2 lbs. cottage cheese
> 2 tbl. brandy

Freeze till it becomes the consistency of sherbet, stirring once. Makes about 5 cups. Serve with wafers and water biscuits.

BUFFET ROQUEFORT SHERBERT

Mix together:

> ⅓ c. cheddar, sharp, and finely grated
> 6 oz. cream cheese
> 1 c. peeled, mashed avocado pulp
> ½ tsp. Worcestershire sauce
> 1 tbl. onion, grated
> ½ tsp. salt
> 1 tsp. lemon juice

AVOCADO CHEESE DIP

HORSERADISH CHEESE DIP

Mix well:

  ½ c. sharp cheddar, finely grated
  6 oz. cream cheese
  ¼ c. sour cream
  ½ tsp. Worcestershire sauce
  1 tsp. onion, finely grated
  1½ tbl. prepared horseradish
  ½ c. beef consommé (the jelling kind)

Refrigerate till served. Makes about 2 cups.

CHIVE-CHEESE DIP

Mix together:

  1 c. cottage cheese
  1 tbl. chives, finely chopped
  ½ c. sour cream
  1 tsp. Worcestershire sauce

Chill for about an hour before serving. Makes about 1½ cups.

COGNAC PATE

Sauté till clear:

  4 tbl. butter
  4 green onions, chopped fine

Add, sauté 10 minutes:

  1 lb. chicken livers

Put in blender. Add, blend till smooth, stirring down as needed:

  1 tsp. salt
  ½ tsp. dry mustard
  ½ tsp. thyme
  ½ tsp. paprika
  ½ tsp. nutmeg

Add, stir together in blender, and pour into a loaf pan:

  1 stick butter
  8 oz. cream cheese
  ½ c. cognac

Chill 24 hours before serving.

PARMESAN BISCUITS

Mix together:

  1 c. flour
  ¼ c. butter
  ½ c. Parmesan cheese, grated
  ¼ tsp. salt

118

Shape into a roll about 1" in diameter. Freeze until semi-firm (about 20 minutes). Cut ¼" thick and place on an ungreased baking sheet. Bake 400°, for 10 minutes. Makes 25.

BUTTERY CHEESE BALL

Mix together:
    ⅓ c. Gorgonzola cheese
    ⅓ c. Parmesan, grated
    ⅓ c. butter
    ½ tsp. Worcestershire sauce
Form into a ball, or use as a spread. Makes 1 cup.

CHEESE SPREAD

Mix together:
    1 c. sharp cheddar cheese, finely grated
    ¼ c. mayonnaise
    1 tbl. lemon juice
    1 tbl. prepared mustard
    1 tbl. grated onion
    1 tsp. Worcestershire sauce
    ¼ c. chopped olives, green or ripe
    2 tbl. chopped parsley or chives
Makes about 2 cups.

CHEDDAR CHEESE MOUSSE

Melt in top of double boiler, over hot, no boiling water:
    ½ lb. sharp cheddar, grated
Heat till smooth and melted. Let cool about 10 minutes. Meanwhile, whip till stiff:
    1 c. heavy cream
    1 tsp. Worcestershire sauce
    1 tsp. kirsch
    ½ tsp. salt
Fold with the cheese and pour into a mold rinsed with cold water. Chill until firm. Unmold and serve with crackers and wafers.

CAMEMBERT MOUSSE

Sprinkle:
    1 pkg. unflavored gelatin
Over:

¼ c. cold water, in a glass cup

Set the cup in a pan of hot water till it is dissolved. Meanwhile, blend till smooth:

½ c. sour cream
6 oz. Camembert
2 oz. blue cheese

Beat in:

1 egg yolk
Dash of salt
The prepared gelatin

Fold in:

1 egg white, beaten stiff
½ c. heavy cream, whipped stiff

Pour into a 2 or 3 cup mold. Refrigerate overnight, serve with crackers and wafers.

AVOCADO CHEESE MOLD

Prepare according to package instructions:

1 3-oz. pkg. lime Jello

Mix in till smooth:

8 oz. (1 cup) cottage cheese, small curd
3 oz. cream cheese
3 oz. Gorgonzola

Fold in:

2 c. avocado pulp (2 to 3 avocados)

Pour into a 2 or 3-cup mold. Refrigerate overnight.

CHEESE SOUP

Place in pan:

3 tbl. butter
1 lg. mild white onion, thinly sliced

Sauté till soft but not brown. Then add:

2 qts. chicken stock
¾ c. parsley, chopped

Heat till simmering barely. Beat in a cup:

2 eggs

Pour a little of the soup mixture (about ½ a cup) into the eggs, then add carefully to the soup, stirring. Add:

½ c. diced mozzarella cheese

Let simmer barely for about fifteen minutes. Sprinkle on top:

¼ c. parsley, chopped
⅓ c. Parmesan, grated

Serve. Makes about 3 quarts of soup.

PORK ROLLS

In a skillet, melt:
> 6 tbl. butter

Add, and sauté till soft but not brown:
> ⅓ c. onion, chopped
> 2 c. sliced mushrooms

Add, off-heat, and mix well:
> ¼ tsp. nutmeg
> ½ tsp. salt
> Dash of pepper
> 1½ c. rice, cooked
> 2 egg yolks

Slice in ½" slices, and trim off all fat:
> 3 lbs. pork loin

Put mixture into each slice, along with:
> 12 thin ¼" by ½" slices of brick cheese

Place in a buttered baking dish and bake at 350° for 45 minutes.

TURKEY ROLLS

In a skillet, sauté till soft but not brown:
> 3 tbl. butter
> 4 green onions, chopped finely
> 1 c. chopped mushrooms

Add:
> 2 tbl. lemon juice
> ½ tsp. salt
> ¼ tsp. pepper

Soak in a bowl:
> 4 stale pieces bread
> ⅓ c. hot cream

Add, mix together. Put an equal portion of mixture into:
> 2-2½ lbs. turkey breast, cut in 12, even,
> thin slices

Roll up rolls neatly, tucking into each roll:
> 12 ¼" by ½" slices of Muenster cheese

Place rolls in buttered baking dish and bake for 20-25 minutes at 350°.

CHICKEN ROLLS

Bone and carefully pound thin:
> 6 chicken breasts

Into each breast, put a portion of this mixture:
> 2 tbl. chives, finely snipped
> 1½ tbl. crumbled roquefort
> ⅓ c. Parmesan, grated
> 1 c. sour cream
> ¼ tsp. salt
> Dash of cayenne

Roll up neatly, secure carefully with a couple of toothpicks, and roll each roll well, in this order in:

> flour
> 1 egg, very well beaten
> fine bread crumbs

Put into well-buttered baking dish and bake at 325° for 30-45 minutes.

MACARONI LOAF

Cook till al denté:

> 1½ lbs. macaroni

Add, and mix well:

> ½ lb. sharp cheddar, grated
> ½ c. milk
> 1 can pimientos, drained and chopped
> 1 tsp. salt
> ½ tsp. pepper
> 2 tbl. onion, chopped finely
> ½-1 c. green onions, chopped finely

Pour into heavily buttered casserole. Bake 350°, 20-30 minutes.

SOUR CREAM ENCHILADAS

Sauté in a skillet:

> ½ lb. ground beef
> 2 green peppers, sliced in thin strips
> 1 lg. onion, sliced thin

Drain, and add:

> 1 c. sharp cheddar, grated

Divide into:

> 1 dozen corn tortillas, sautéed till soft

Fold up. Put in an ovenproof dish for 5-10 minutes at 375° (until cheese melts). Top with sour cream and serve.

GREEN NOODLE SOUFFLE

Beat until well mixed:

> ¼ lb. unsalted butter
> 1 c. sour cream
> 1 c. ricotta or cottage cheese
> 3 tbl. sugar
> 4 eggs
> 2 tbl. lemon juice

Fold in:

> 8 oz. green broad noodles, cooked al denté
> 2 black truffles, sliced thinly

Pour into a buttered 1½-cup soufflé or casserole. Bake 350° for 25-30 minutes. Serves 6.

Mix together:

> 1 c. cottage cheese
> ½ c. sour cream
> 1 tbl. chives, finely chopped
> ½ c. Parmesan, grated

Mix in with:

> 1 lb. broad noodles, cooked al denté

Pour into a buttered casserole and top with:

> ⅔ c. buttered bread crumbs

Bake 350° for 30 minutes. Serves 6.

NOODLE CASSEROLE

In a small skillet, melt:

> 2 tbl. butter

Stir in:

> 2 tbl. flour

Stir in slowly:

> ¾ c. milk
> salt
> pepper

Beat in alternately:

> 4 egg yolks
> 1 c. sharp cheddar, grated

Fold in:

> 6 egg whites, beaten stiff
> 1 4½-oz. can of crab, drained

CRAB-CHEESE SOUFFLE

Clean thoroughly:

> 1 lb. spinach

Cook over high heat with just the moisture clinging to the leaves. Drain, chop very finely. Add:

CLAM FILLING

                    salt
                    pepper
          1 6-oz. can of minced clams, drained
          1 pt. ricotta
          ½ c. Parmesan cheese, grated
Use to stuff pasta or in casseroles.

STUFFED POTATOES

Bake some good baking potatoes. When they are done, cut off part of the top, scoop out the pulp, and mash in a bowl with:
          lemon juice (about 1 tsp. per cup of potatoes)
          salt and pepper to taste
          grated onion (about 1 tsp. per cup)
          grated cheese (cheddar and Parmesan are particularly
             good. Use in whatever proportion you want.)
Now stir this mixture up with:
          sliced, cooked hot dogs
          fried bacon bits
          drained tuna fish
          seasoned, cooked, and drained hamburger
Or whatever you want. Sprinkle with paprika, scoop the mixture back into the potato shells and place back under broiler just until cheese melts.

BAKED TOMATOES

Cut off the top and a small section of the bottom of:
          6 lg. tomatoes
Carefully scoop out part of the pulp. Dice this into a bowl and add:
          1 tsp. wine vinegar
          1 tsp. chives, finely chopped
            salt
            pepper
Grate:
          ¼ c. Swiss cheese
Toss with:
          ½ c. bread crumbs
Mix with other ingredients, and put into tomato shells. Dot each tomato shell with:
          ½ tsp. butter
Put under broiler until hot and lightly toasted.

BAKED EGGS AND CHEESE

Into 6 ramekins (small ovenproof baking cups), place in each one, in this order:

>   1 tsp. butter
>   1 tbl. cream
>   1 tbl. grated cheddar
>   1 egg
>   salt
>   pepper
>   1 tbl. cream to top

Place the ramekins in a larger pan with an inch or two of boiling water
Bake at 375° for 8-12 minutes. Serve on toast. Makes 6 servings.

CHEESE CORNMEAL MUFFINS

Mix together in a bowl:

>   1¼ c. white flour
>   1 c. yellow cornmeal
>   4 tsp. baking powder
>   ½ tsp. salt
>   2 tbl. sugar

Add, beat just until mixed:

>   1 egg, beaten
>   1 c. milk
>   ½ c. grated cheddar
>   4 tbl. shortening, melted

Pour into greased muffin tins till muffin cups are about ⅔ full of batter
Bake for 25 minutes at 425°.

BLUE CHEESE-BUTTERMILK DRESSING

Beat together till smooth:

>   1 c. mayonnaise
>   1 tsp. monosodium glutamate
>   1½ tsp. chopped parsley
>   1 tbl. blue cheese

Slowly add, stirring till smooth:

>   1 c. buttermilk

Refrigerate a couple of hours before serving.

BLUE CHEESE-PIMIENTO DRESSING

Mix together:

    1 c. mayonnaise
    1 c. sour cream
    2 tbl. blue cheese
    1 can pimientos, drained and chopped finely
    ¼ tsp. salt
    dash of pepper
    ½ tsp. sugar

REUBEN GRILL

Mix together:

    ½ c. mayonnaise
    1 tbl. prepared mustard

Spread evenly on:

    8 slices dark rye bread

On four slices of bread, evenly put first:

    4 slices Swiss cheese
    ½ lb. corned beef, thinly sliced

On the other four slices of bread, put:

    1 c. sauerkraut, drained well

Butter the outside of each sandwich, both sides, with:

    1½ tsp. butter

Grill on both sides till lightly toasted. Makes 4 sandwiches.

MONACO GRILL

On:

    8 slices light rye bread

Spread:

    mustard mayonnaise (see Reuben Grill)

Then place:

    1 slice Swiss cheese (8 slices all together)

Divide evenly:

    ½ lb. baked turkey breast, thinly sliced
    ½ lb. baked ham, thinly sliced

Butter the outside of each sandwich with:

    1½ tsp. butter

Grill until toasted on each side. Makes 4 sandwiches.

GRILLED BACON, TOMATO, AND CHEESE

For each sandwich to be made, spread its inside lightly with:

    mayonnaise

On:

        firm white bread

Then add:

        1 *thin* slice mild cheddar

        thin slices of tomato

      3 or 4 slices of crisp bacon

Butter outside of each sandwich with:

        1-1½ tsp. butter

Grill until the cheese melts.

Use:

THE (ALL-CHEESE) FROSTED SANDWICH LOAF

        1 loaf firm, white bread

Trim neatly of all crusts and slice lengthwise 4 times to yield 5 long slices of bread. On the bottom slice put a mixture of:

        2 oz. cream cheese

        2 tbl. pimiento, finely chopped

      ½ c. walnuts, chopped finely

        milk, if desired

On the next slice, put a mixture of:

        1 c. cooked chicken livers, finely chopped

        1 tsp. chives, finely chopped

      ¼ tsp. nutmeg

        2 oz. cream cheese

        milk, if desired

On the next slice, put a mixture of:

      ½ c. finely chopped green olives

      ½ tsp. Worcestershire sauce

      ⅔ c. mozzarella, finely grated (smoked if possible)

        milk, if desired

On the next slice, put a mixture of:

        1 small can baby shrimp, drained

        1 tsp. soy sauce

        2 oz. cream cheese

        milk, if desired

Spread top and side of assembled loaf with whipped cream cheese (*see* next).

Whip together till fluffy:

WHIPPED CREAM CHEESE

        8 oz. cream cheese

        2 tbl. sour cream

        1 tbl. milk

        2 tbl. sugar

        pinch of salt

STUFFED PEARS For each halved pear, fill cavity with an equal mixture of:

> butter
> Gorgonzola cheese

Add about:

> 1 tsp. pulverized almonds

Top with a few sliced almonds and run under broiler for a few minutes to heat up.

HOT FRUIT AU GRATIN Mix together in an ovenproof dish:

> 1 1-lb. can Bartlett pears, drained
> 1 1-lb. can cling peaches, drained
> 1 1-lb. can bing cherries, drained
> 1 1-lb. can apricots, drained
> juice of one lemon
> ¼ c. honey
> 1 c. Swiss cheese, grated

Bake 350° for 25-30 minutes. Serve hot with sour cream.

APPLE CHEESE TART Peel, core, and slice lengthwise around the apple:

> 6-7 tart apples

Add:

> ½ c. sugar

Put aside for about ½ an hour. Meanwhile, make the crust. Mix together in a bowl:

> 1¼ c. flour
> 1 tsp. salt

Cut in:

> ½ c. shortening

Stir in:

> just enough cold water to hold together

Roll out. Enough for 1 2-crust pie. Arrange the apple slices neatly and artistically in the pie shell, layering every 3 or 4 rows with:

> a small slice of well-aged cheddar cheese

Dot with about:

> ⅔ stick of butter

Sprinkle over:

> ⅔ c. sugar

Bake 350° for 45 minutes.

Form into a ball:

        8 oz. Neufchatel cheese

        ⅓ c. coarsely chopped glacé cherries

CREAM CHEESE
WITH FRUIT

Make graham cracker crust for 8 or 9″ pie plate:

        1½ c. graham cracker crumbs

        ⅓ c. melted butter

        ¼ c. sugar

Mix together, and press into place. Meanwhile prepare:

        1 6-oz. pkg. orange Jello

With:

        1 c. hot water

        1 c. orange juice

Beat in:

        8 oz. cream cheese

Whip until stiff:

        ½ c. cream

          Sugar to taste

Fold together with:

        ½ c. sour cream

        1 tbl. orange peel

        1 tbl. orange liqueur or 1 tsp. orange flavoring

Refrigerate until firm, about 3-4 hours.

ORANGE
NO-BAKE
CHEESECAKE

Beat together:

        1 lb. cream cheese

        2 eggs

        1 c. sugar

        1 tsp. vanilla

        2 tbl. lemon juice

        1 tbl. lemon rind, shredded

Pour into a graham cracker crust, made by simply buttering an 8 or 9″ pie plate heavily and pressing in ½ c. of graham cracker crumbs. Put into a larger pan filled with hot water and bake at 325° for 1½ hours. Then turn off the oven and let the cheesecake remain in the oven for another ½ hour.

A SIMPLE AND
DELICIOUS
CHEESECAKE

COTTAGE CHEESE CHEESECAKE

Beat together:

    1 pt. cottage cheese
    1 c. sour cream
    1 c. sugar
    2 tbl. cornstarch
    dash of salt
    2 egg yolks
    1 tsp. vanilla
    1 tsp. lemon peel

Fold in:

    1 c. sultana raisins
    2 egg whites, beaten stiff
    ¼ c. blanched almonds, sliced

Pour into an 8 or 9" pie plate lined with this crust:

    1 c. flour
    2 oz. cream cheese
    1 tbl. butter

Bake 450° for 10 minutes, and at 350° for 45 minutes.

RICH CREAM CHEESE FUDGE

Mix together:

    3 oz. cream cheese
    1 tbl. cream

Stir in:

    2 c. unsifted powdered sugar
    2 sq. unsweetened chocolate, melted
    1 tsp. vanilla
    ½ c. black walnuts, coarsely chopped
    ½ c. maraschino cherries, drained and finely chopped

Press into a lightly buttered 8" square pan, chill till firm. Makes 1 lb.

Chapter 13

More About Cheese

For those who are basically more interested in self-sufficiency than cheesemaking, it should be stated that the only thing really needed to make some cheeses is milk. Certain cheeses can always be allowed to acidify to the point where they will form a curd through acidity alone.

Perhaps an explanation of a few terms is in order. Rennin is an enzyme found in the stomach of calves, lambs, kids and similar animals. Rennet, on the other hand, can be the enzyme rennin or any of a number of other substances that will accomplish the same thing. Calcium chloride, lemon or lime juice, lactic acid, and some plant sources can also be used to coagulate milk.

It seems that in the latter category we are considerably behind our ancestors. In some areas, from all indications, plants were the chief agents used to clabber milk, but after a time these methods fell into disuse until now they are almost wholly forgotten. About all that remains of this knowledge is obscure references in all-but-forgotten books.

One plant that can be used for a rennet is stinging nettle (*Urtica gracilis*). Boil a pound of stinging nettle in just enough water to cover. Boil for twenty to thirty minutes and then strain the liquid off. Add as much salt as will dissolve, with agitation, in the warm liquid. How much of this infusion will be needed to coagulate the milk is difficult o estimate because of the variability of its strength and the acidity of

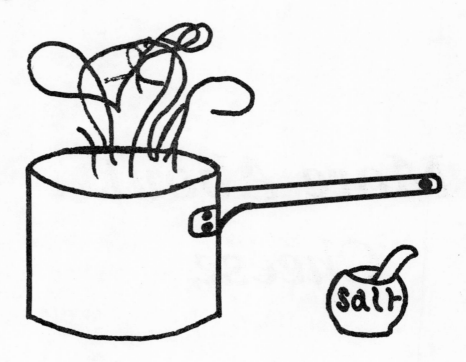

the milk. A good average starting point would be one-half cup of net-tle infusion per gallon of milk. A word of caution would be in order at this point. The salt in the nettle infusion will inhibit the ripening char-acteristics of the curd which makes it unsuitable for cheddar and other cheeses that are ripened a significant length of time after the rennet has been added. It works best for cheeses that are salted shortly after the curd has formed. Remember also that the curd already has some salt in it so take this into consideration during the salting step.

The dried flowers of the Cardus species of sunflower can also be used. Dry the blossoms and grind them to a powder with a mortar and pestle. Dissolve a couple of teaspoons of the powder in ½ cup of water and then add the infusion to the milk the same as if using a rennet solution.

The acid produced by the acid-producing organisms in starters will, when strong enough, be sufficient to cause the milk to curdle. In making some cheeses—Queso Blanco, for instance—the starter can be eliminated and a nontoxic acid such as lemon juice can be substituted for lactic acid in coagulating milk. The important thing to remember is that the lower the temperature, the more the acid required to coagu-late the curd. The higher the temperature, the less acid required. When using the milk-fermenting or milk-ripening cultures, remember that too high a temperature will kill the microorganism. Cultures that use yogurt or other heat-loving cultures, however, are able to stand higher temperatures than the buttermilk cultures without impairment.

The cottage cheese industry has found an economical coagulator in the "Cornell Commercial Coagulator" and during periods of shortage pepsin has been used with fairly good results. Rumor is that in ancient times butterwort was used to coagulate milk. Zeus was supposed to have eaten a cheese made by coagulating milk with the juice of figs. Papain and bromelin from papaya and pineapple have been used, but with inferior results. There are various other microbial sources of substances that seem to do a fairly good job, but they are not yet of any practical interest to the home cheesemaker. Regular rennet from animal sources seems to be the most effective, both as far as the quality of the curd is concerned and in the curd's ability to rid itself of whey. This failure of the curd to expel whey is the major cause of "wet acid." If for some reason you don't want to use commercial rennet, you can make your own top-quality rennet.

A young lamb, calf or kid is needed. It must be in the suckling stage and it should be too young to eat grass or other plant foods. To make the rennet, the animal will have to be killed so, if at all possible, select one otherwise of little value or one anyway scheduled for slaughter. An animal with some defect might be a good candidate. After the animal is killed remove the stomach. Note that rennin is taken from the fourth stomach of a calf—this will be the biggest of the four compartments of the stomach. After the stomach is removed it will have to be treated so that flies and bacteria will not attack it until it has been dried. Our ancestors used the simple expedient of just rolling the stomach in the ashes of a campfire to protect it with the lye found in the ashes. After it has been covered with ashes, hang it up to dry away from animals and other things that could contaminate it. A warm, dry breeze or a good airy place would help do the job. When dried, the milk (the only thing that the animal has eaten) will have been reduced to a brownish powder. Open up the stomach and remove this powder. This contains rennin, which is used in making cheese. As is to be expected of an enzyme (which is nothing more than an organic catalyst), it will break down if exposed to too high a heat. It should be stored in a cool, dark place. When rennin is heated higher than 102° F it starts breaking down. To use, take a teaspoon and grind it up thoroughly. Remove ⅛ teaspoon and put it in a cup. Add a drop of water and mix it in, then add more water, a drop at a time, until it has formed a thick paste. Now add cool or lukewarm water to dissolve it just as though using a rennet tablet. This will be enough rennet to coagulate 8 to 12 gallons of milk.

Acidity

The amount of acid developed by the starter at the time the rennet is added, the time the curd is cut, the length of and temperature at which the curd is cooked, and the time at which the whey is drained are some of the significant and important things that can be regulated in the cheesemaking process. Given an active starter and following the directions for the individual cheeses, you should get good results because the milk should develop the required acidity in the time set aside for each step. For those who like to keep a very close eye on the cheesemaking process as the professional cheesemakers do, there is a way to directly measure the acidity with very little trouble.

You will need:
  a bottle of (n)/9 (ninth normal)
    solution of caustic soda
  1 burette
  1 pipette
  phenophthalein
  small clear or white container
  stirring rod

The object of this test is to determine the percentage of acid in the milk or whey. A specific amount of milk or whey is put in a flask or similar container, then a few drops of phenolphthalein solution are added to the milk. This is an indicator; when the milk loses its acidity and becomes basic, it will become pink. The amount of basic solution is measured and with some simple math (to be explained shortly) the percentage of acid is determined.

Begin by filling the pipette with 10cc of milk or whey and putting it in the dish. Now add a few drops of phenolphthalein to the milk. Stir it in. Now fill the burette to the top of the marker. The burette should be marked in tenths of a cubic centimeter so that you may accurately measure the amount of caustic soda used. Slowly add the caustic soda to the milk or whey containing the phenophthalein. Add just a little and then stir it in. The milk or whey will turn pink immediately around where the solution has been added and then turn colorless as it is stirred in. Keep adding the caustic soda solution to the liquid being tested. Just before the acid is neutralized, the pink will spread almost throughout, but with vigorous stirring it will turn the original color again. The next little amount of caustic soda will turn it a permanent pink. Read the amount of caustic soda solution used off the burette.

Since one cubic centimeter of the (n)/9 solution will neutralize 0.01 of a gram of acid, multiply 0.01 times the number of cubic centimeters of caustic soda used. This will give the amount of acid present in ten cubic centimeters of milk or whey. To get the percentage it will be necessary to know the quantity of acid in 100cc. This can be found by multiplying the amount of acid found in 10cc by 10. Thus the formula will be the number of cc of caustic soda used *times* 0.01 *times* 10. If it takes 2.1cc of caustic soda to neutralize the acid in 10ccs of whey, the calculation would look like this:

$$2.1 \times 0.01 \times 10 = 0.21 \text{ percent acid}$$

If it took 1.8cc caustic soda to neutralize the acid in 10cc of milk or whey the problem would be this:

$$1.8 \times 0.01 \times 10 = 0.18 \text{ percent acid}$$

It might seem just a little complicated at first but after a few tests it will become very easy.

The acidity measurement just given is a direct measurement of the acidity of the whey or the original milk. There are also ways of measuring the acidity of the curd. Most of the measurements are either indirect (that is, they measure the acidity of the whey and then from experience it is known about what the acidity of the curd will be) or quite expensive. There is a device, for instance, that measures the flow of an electrical current through the curd. The amount of electrical current is dependent on the amount of acidity in the curd.

Another simple and inexpensive acid measurement is called the "hot iron test." This takes advantage of the fact that acid acts as a softening agent in the cheese curd. The greater the degree of acid, the softer the curd becomes, and the longer the strings of acid that will be produced. Begin by heating a piece of pipe or a large spike in an open flame. Lift up a handful of drained curd and press it against the hot iron. At first it is a little difficult to get the pipe the right temperature. All that is needed is to touch the curd to the hot iron. If the iron is too cold the curd will not melt. If it is too hot the curd will melt all right, but it won't stick. Until you get the hang of it, just heat the tip of the iron too hot and then move the curd back toward the cool end. When the temperature is just right the cheese will stick to the hot iron and will string out in threads. By measuring the length of the tiny threads you can get a relative idea of how much acid is present. This test is an ideal one to go along with the cheese chart at the end of the second chapter. If you have good results when the whey is drained from the curd and the strings are a certain length, then on a particular day the acid strings are not as long as they normally would be using the time chart, it would indicate a slow starter. Instead of producing a cheese that wouldn't be up to your normal standards you could let it ripen just a little more in the cooker before draining the curd. The higher the acid the longer the strings of acid, up to a point, and then the test no longer works.

This test is mentioned several places in this book to aid in telling when the curd is ready for some particularly delicate procedure. When the acidity reaches 0.20 percent it will form strings ⅛-inch long, by the way. When the milk or whey acidity has increased enough to taste, it indicates an acidity of 0.30 percent or, if your taste is sensitive, just slightly less.

When Things Go Wrong

This is a part of the book I hope you never have to use, but occasionally—especially at first—things can go wrong. Here are some of the most common cheese defects and some of the things that can be done about them.

Off-flavors: Often the off-flavor comes from the milk itself. Flavors can be absorbed from the foods the dairy animal has eaten, foods such as wild onions or garlic. Odors can be absorbed by the milk, itself, directly from things near it. The most dangerous form of off-flavors and odors comes from microbial contamination.

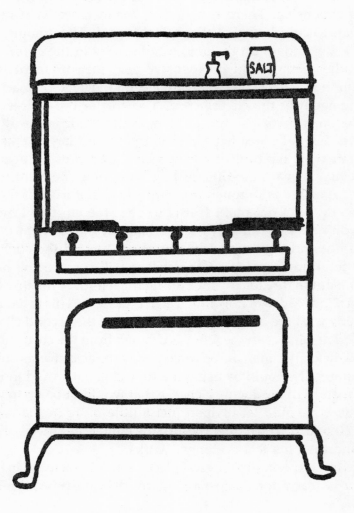

The cure involves being especially careful throughout the whole cheesemaking process. Keep dairy animals away from plants likely to taint the milk. Keep the milk away from odiferous substances. Usually the latter are absorbed when the milk is stored in a cooler where other types of food are stored and the milk picks up their odor. Cream and other forms of butterfat are especially vulnerable to this form of contamination. Fats of all kinds easily pick up odors; because of this characteristic they are often used by amateur perfumemakers to capture the essence of summer flowers for later enjoyment.

Off-flavors and odors have a very useful function. They are nature's way of saying that something is wrong. In cheeses they often indicate some form of contamination. Indications include fruity or yeasty tastes or other odd flavors.

Holes: Often the curd is gassy. That is to say it has gas holes in the curd. These holes may be very small and numerous or appear as large bubbles that give the curd a misshapen, bloated appearance.

To prevent this, check all sanitation procedures. Make sure that all utensils and containers are sterilized and clean. If you suspect the milk, allow a little to sour by itself and see if any of the faults become evident in the soured milk. Check all sanitation procedures used with the dairy animals.

It could be the starter. Don't save the starter out of the whey. Don't allow the starter to become too acidic or too old. If there is any doubt about the starter obtain a fresh start. It is much less expensive to buy a new starter at the outset rather than lose several gallons of milk by using a poor one and then having to buy a fresh starter anyway. If the starter is not active enough the milk just will not ripen as fast as it should and undesirable forms of bacteria may gain the upper hand.

Sour, bitter cheese: This is a sign of too much acid. This can be "wet acid" caused by cooking the curd too fast, trapping whey inside the curd. It can be caused by adding too much starter or, in some cases, leaving the starter in so that it develops too much acid. A weak and pasty curd is another sign of wet acid.

Mottled and/or greasy surface: This is one of the faults found in cheddar. It can be caused by bruising the curd. This can occur when the curd is cut or milled, or by applying too much pressure too soon.

Checked surfaces: This is usually caused by allowing the cheese to dry out. This can happen if the humidity is allowed to fall too low. To cure, wipe with a damp cloth. If mold is a problem, wipe with a cloth that has been moistened with salt water. Increase the humidity and, if the cheese is one that can be paraffined without harming its characteristics, do so. An alternate method is to rub the surface with an organic oil such as olive oil.

Mold: This is a problem that all kitchen cheesemakers face at one time or another. The mold can be scraped off the surface. Perhaps the humidity is too high. Salt water in varying concentrations can be wiped on the surface of the cheese with a moistened cloth. If the mold is very persistent the cause could very well be in the curing chamber. If the mold-ripened cheeses have been cured in a chamber, they are undoubtedly full of mold spores. This can be good, of course, if you are going to be constantly making Stiltons or perhaps Camemberts. In some areas where these cheeses are made right along, they don't even bother inoculating the cheeses with any special organisms; they are picked up unaided from their surroundings.

Trying to ripen a cheddar in a curing chamber that has just ripened a Gorgonzola can be a problem if you don't want to end up with a blue cheddar. To avoid this, buy some sulphur and burn it in the curing chamber after it has first been thoroughly moistened with water.

Where to Find it

In general, the idea has been to keep things as simple as possible and avoid the expense of having to buy any special products and equipment from outside sources. Still, in isolated areas or similar circumstances where the things needed are not available locally, it might be an advantage to purchase by mail. If you feel it would be more practical to obtain the things needed directly from a commercial source, here is a short list of suppliers.

Institut Rosell Inc.
1000, boul. Industriel Chambly
Quebec, Canada J3L 3H9

Institut Rosell has the basic cultures plus the molds and bacteria needed to make the cheeses in this book. They supply them on an industrial scale but will also provide them for home use.

Chr. Hansen's Laboratory, Inc.
9015 West Maple Street
Milwaukee, Wisconsin 53214

This company's main business is with the commercial dairies but they will supply others with the same cultures if so desired. A price list can be obtained by writing to them. The above is their American address but they have offices world-wide.

Homecrafts
111 Stratford Center,
Winston-Salem, North Carolina 27104

Homecrafts is a company that will supply cheesemaking equipment and other things useful in making cheeses in the kitchen. They also distribute a catalog.

There are other sources for cheesemaking supplies, but most of them cater almost exclusively to the commercial dairy trade. Most of them will only sell certain items to the kitchen cheesemaker. Part of the reason for this is that the quantities they sell are measured for thousands of gallons of milk and costs would be prohibitive to the casual cheesemaker.

Index

3